101 Vacation Rental Tips

LifeTips Book Series

By Lynne R. Christen
Travel Guru
LifeTips

LifeTips
Move Up In Life.
LifeTips Book Series
Boston, Massachusetts

LIFETIPS PRESIDENT: Byron White
BOOK SERIES EDITOR: Melanie Nayer

All inquires should be addressed to:

LifeTips.com, Inc.
101 Book Series
One First Avenue
Building 34, Suite 200
Charlestown, MA 02129
(617) 886-9001
http://www.LifeTips.com

International Standard Book No. 978-1-60275-003-6

Table of Contents

A Note from the Editor

For many people, a vacation is something we dream about taking but never get around to actually booking the trip. Between the grinding phone calls, the back-to-back meetings, his office party, her cocktail event, the weekend carpools and the family pet's vet appointment, you can barely find the time to make it to the gym for 15-minute escape in the steam room. But you need a vacation. Correction: you deserve a vacation.

Today's travelers are savvier than before and demand more in terms of lifestyle, luxury and convenience. The perfect vacation rental offers it all. Lynne Christen's love of travel led to writing *Travel Wisdom-Tips, Tools, and Tactics for All Travelers*, named Runner-Up Best 2004 Travel Book by North American Travel Journalists Association. Lynne has traveled to 47 countries, throughout the United States and on 20 cruises, so with her tips, you're on your way to planning the perfect vacation.

From a rental house in the Hamptons to a vacation home in the woods, with these tips you can travel safely, and more often.

Happy Travels!

Melanie Nayer
Editor, LifeTips

A Note from the Author

During my 40+ years traveling the world, I have stayed at accommodations ranging from tiny bed and breakfasts to luxury resorts and cruise ships. Several years ago, my husband and I discovered the advantages of staying in vacation home rentals versus traditional hotels. Since that time most of our vacation rentals around the world have been perfect; we wouldn't change a thing.

A vacation home rental allows us to briefly become "locals" rather than tourists. We tend to slow down our pace and experience more of the lifestyles of our destination. A vacation rental is a good base for exploring the immediate area, venturing forth on entertaining and educational day trips knowing we will be returning to the luxury and privacy of "home" at night. Invariably, we meet interesting people in neighborhood markets and sidewalk cafes that we might not encounter in a traditional hotel setting and some of these acquaintances become friends.

One of the greatest pleasures about travel writing is the opportunity to share travel discoveries and unique travel experiences. Thus, I wrote 101 Tips for Vacation Home Rentals. Every effort was made to provide accurate and up-to-date information about many aspects of vacation home rental markets. However, change is a constant in the travel industry and it pays to double check sources for recent updates or changes at destinations and accommodations. Now, come along with me for tips on vacation rentals at some of my favorite travel destinations.

Lynne Christen
LifeTips Travel Guru

1| Best Time to Vacation in Cape Cod

For many visitors Cape Cod is a year-round destination. Each season holds special delights and activities.

Summer season is considered the high season. Vacation rental rates are the highest and the beaches are crowded as vacationers seek to escape the heat of the city.

Fall season is longer than most of New England. Accommodation rates drop shortly after Labor Day. Ocean waters cool down slowly and days are temperate allowing visitors to enjoy the beaches well into November.

Winter in Cape Cod tends to be somewhat milder than inland.

Spring comes slowly to the Cape with chilly nights and frequent fog. Off-season rates make travel to Cape Cod during the fall, winter and spring a bargain.

Note: Always check the weather when planning any vacation. Dressing appropriately for the local climate makes travel more pleasurable. In Cape Cod, even summer evenings may turn chilly and a light jacket or wrap is necessary. In winter, think layers rather than bulk and a winter beach walk followed by a warm drink in front of a cozy fire is the perfect combination of exhilaration and relaxation.

2| Things to Do on a Cape Cod Vacation

Although most visitors enjoy leisurely days sunning, swimming and strolling sandy beaches lulled by the sound of the surf; there is plenty to do off the beach in Cape Cod. Here's just a sample of the treats in store for you:

· Spend a morning or afternoon on a whale watching excursion.

· Adventurous types go for windsurfing, sea kayaking, diving or deep-sea fishing.

· Cape Cod abounds with specialty and antique shops, golf courses, museums and sightseeing tours.

· View Cape Cod dunes, marshes, towns and villages with a ride on the Cape Cod Central Railroad. You can enjoy a three-hour ride with a five-course meal on the dinner train.

· Meet the "ghosts" of Jonathan Hatch and friends at the Falmouth Ghost Tour at the Old Burying Ground off Locust Street.

· Catch a performance at the Barnstable Comedy Club, one of the oldest, longest-running community theaters in Massachusetts.

Get the idea? It's never boring at the beach in Cape Cod.

3| Cape Cod Special Events Fill the Calendar

There's always something going on in Cape Cod. The locals love to celebrate year round with festivals, races, parades, tours tourneys and shows. Check local calendars and plan your Cape Cod vacation around special event that pique your interest.

Summer brings the **Annual Kitchen Tour in** Cotuit; a self-guided tour of five or six beautiful homes in the Cotuit/Osterville area featuring artists painting on location, crafts demonstrations, floral displays and raffles. Try your hand at making luscious desserts at the Sandwich Strawberry Festival. Celebrate the 4th of July across the Cape. Ride the Midway at the old-fashioned Barnstable County Fair.

Fall is everyone's favorite time of year in Cape Cod. Don't miss the **Annual Bourne Scallop Fest in** Buzzards Bay in September. It's the largest scallop fest on the East Coast. Art lovers are sure to find a treasure at the **Annual Art Auction** in Provincetown. Give your libido a boost at the **Oyster Festival** in Hyannis in October. The Pilgrims played a significant part in Cape Cod history and Thanksgiving reflects this heritage.

Winter brings weeks of holidays lights and celebrations and **First Night** celebrations usher in the New Year around the Cape. Although spring comes slowly to the Cape, it brings a **Daffodil Festival** and dozens of garden and home tours.

4| Cape Cod Weddings Spell Romance

There are many locations in Cape Cod that lead to happily-after-after. Whether you want a barefoot beach wedding, an intimate garden soiree or a formal affair for a hundred or so of your closest friends, you will find the perfect venue for every budget in Cape Cod. Use these additional tips to ensure that the big day goes off without a hitch:

- Choose your wedding theme or style. The options are endless in Cape Cod.
- Go traditional or trendy. This day is all about your hopes and dreams.
- Choose your wedding date as soon as possible. The Cape is a popular wedding destination. Spring or fall weddings are lovely on Cape Cod.
- Consider a wedding date during the shoulder or off-season to avoid summer crowds and save money. It is easy for wedding expenses to get out of control.
- Decide on a wedding budget and stick to it. Fortunately, the variety and proximity of Cape Cod house, cottage and condo rentals makes it easy for family and guests to find accommodations.
- Hire a local wedding coordinator. Planning a wedding is exciting, but also stressful. A local wedding coordinator can save money and handle the myriad of details necessary to ensure that your wedding is perfect.

And don't forget, Cape Cod is a wonderfully romantic honeymoon destination!

5| Delectable Dining in Cape Cod

From rustic waterfront seafood shanties to romantic fine dining, Cape Cod boasts over 1,000 eateries between Provincetown on the outermost tip of the Cape and the Canal. According to the Chamber of Commerce, you can eat breakfast, lunch and dinner at a different spot each day and never dine at the same place twice in a year. No matter what your taste buds crave, there is great dining close by. For fine dining, check out **Twenty Eight Atlantic** in Chatham, **The Captain Linnell House** in Orleans or the Sunday Brunch at **Coonamessett Inn** in Falmouth. Pack a picnic. Go gourmet; there are plenty of markets and restaurants to provide fancy fixings. Or, keep it simple; a hot dog and a cold beer never taste better than on the beach. Also, no New England trip is complete without digging into a traditional Cape Cod Clambake.

Local restaurants offer versions of clambakes. Combine a clambake and a sunset cruise with a Cape Cod Clambake Cruise. Or, throw your own old-fashioned shindig for family and friends at your Cape Cod cottage.

Here's a sample Clambake menu:

1-1¼lb Fresh Native Lobster
Farm Fresh Corn on the Cob
Drawn Butter & Seasoned Broth
Chatham Steamed Clams
Linqucia Sweet Sausage
New Potatoes
Steamed Onions
Sweet Potatoes
Cape Cod Cookie

6| Finding the Best Cape Cod Beach Rental

There is no shortage of great **Cape Cod vacation rentals**; however, it pays to plan ahead to score the perfect rental especially during the summer season and on holiday weekends. Cape Cod locals offer these tips:

- Begin your search by searching the Internet using targeted phrases such as "Cape Cod summer rentals" or "vacationing in Cape Cod."
- Study vacation rental properties online to ensure that the accommodations, location and rental policies meet your needs. If being on the beachfront is important, you may be disappointed with a property blocks away from the shore.
- Don't rely only on Web site photographs. Contact the property owner to clarify questions and ensure availability of personal needs and preferences.
- Get rental contracts in writing. Examine cancellation clauses and restrictions.

7| It's Easy to Fall in Love with Cape Cod

Cape Cod is a scenic peninsula on the coast of Massachusetts. It is connected to the mainland by two highway bridges across the Cape Cod Canal. There is also ferry service between Provincetown - a city on the tip of Cape Cod - and Boston. Cape Cod is made up of four distinctive sections. The **Upper Cape** is the section closest to the mainland. The **Mid-Cape** area is home of Falmouth, known for the Woods Hole Oceanographic Institution and other research groups. The **Lower Cape** is the most northern and narrow part of the Cape. The **Outer Cape** is the outermost part and is known for beautiful beaches like Nauset Light Beach in Eastham.

Whether you are looking for the perfect destination for a family reunion, a guys' golf outing, a girlfriends' getaway or a romantic retreat, there is a Cape Cod vacation rental to match your taste and budget. Picture a five bedroom fine home on the beach-front. Imagine an evening by the fire in a romantic bungalow for two. Like upscale accommodations? Check into a luxurious condominium packed with perks. Stay for the weekend, a week, a month or the season and discover how easy it is in the words of Patti Page to "Fall in Love with Old Cape Cod."

8| It's a Whale of a Good Time

A whale watching trip is a must-do in Cape Cod. If you have never been up close to one of these majestic creatures - close enough to feel the mist as they surface and blow and hear their songs in the deep, you have missed an experience of a lifetime. Cape Cod's Stellwagon Bank is a marine sanctuary (nine miles off Provincetown) for whales. There are numerous whale watching cruise excursions and most have naturalists aboard to guide the way. You can expect to see humpback, finback and right whales and you may be lucky enough to catch a view of a mother nurturing her calf.

Cruises operate from mid-April through mid-October and prices average $30-$35 for the four hour trip. Some of the most popular Whale Watch boats include: the Dolphin Fleet, Ranger V and Portuguese Princess out of Provincetown or Hyannis and Hyannis Whale Watcher Cruises out of Barnstable Harbor. Notes: Dress warmly in layers. It is always cooler on the water, especially in the early spring and fall months. And...don't forget your camera.

9| Popular Provincetown Draws Repeat Visitors

Provincetown, called **P-Town** by locals, is located in the outermost point of Cape Cod. Known as an artist's haven, there are treasures awaiting you in the eclectic galleries along Commercial Street. Over 30 miles of beach front and an active historic seaport make Provincetown the perfect launching point for whale watching. History buffs appreciate the **Pilgrim Monument** (the tallest granite structure in America) and **Provincetown Heritage Museum**. And, when the sun goes down, nightlife is Provincetown is anything but boring.

Provincetown is not a day-trip kind of place. There's way too much to enjoy. Fortunately finding perfect accommodations is easy. Provincetown vacation home rentals are as diverse as the town itself. For example, couples seeking a romantic retreat fall in love with **The Tree House** with its amazing unobstructed views of the harbor.

Rent in July and August is $1,700 per week. Shoulder or off season rates are a bargain at $150 per night for a three night minimum stay. For a group of family or friends, nearby **Treetops Duplex** sits upon the top of its own hill in Provincetown's East End and is surrounded by private gardens and breath-taking views of the entire Provincetown Harbor. Off-season rates start September 9th at $200 per night (three night minimum) or $1,700 per week. It is said that no one forgets their first visit to Provincetown and no one makes the first visit the last.

10| What to Expect in Cape Cod Rental Rates

There are literally hundreds of Cape Cod vacation rentals; so finding the right property for your budget should not be a problem. Before beginning your search for the perfect property, determine how much you want to spend for a weekend or a week's stay. For instance, a beautiful waterfront getaway on **Mill Pond** in Chatham features three bedrooms, two baths and comes with use of a canoe and paddle boat for fun on the water. Weekly rental rates range from $3,500 per week in the summer to $1,700 in the early fall. In Brewster, an ocean edge resort condo with two bedrooms and two baths and all the comforts of home and more rents for as low as $1,400 per week.

Note: Multi-bedroom homes and condos make it easy to share travel costs with family or friends. Also, if your travel schedule is flexible, you can save travel dollars by renting during the "shoulder" season in late spring or early fall. Cuddle up by the fireplace during chilly nights and enjoy temperate days on Cape Cod beaches.

11| Best Time to Travel to the Caribbean

Anytime is a *good* time to vacation in the Caribbean. The climate year-round is warmed by sunlight and cooled by sea breezes. Of course, when Old Man Winter is wreaking havoc in frigid climates, tropical appeal is at its peak. In the Caribbean, the high season runs from December through mid-April. Although beachfront vacations rentals cost more at this time, with due diligence you can still find ways to save money on your vacation. During the off or shoulder seasons, greatly reduced accommodations and air travel offer savings as much as 50% less than in high season. For instance, Air Jamaica, a leading Caribbean airline, offers vacation packages starting as low as $599 for three-night stays including airfare from major cities in the U.S.

Also, a search of Caribbean vacation rentals on numerous islands uncovers summer beach vacation villa rentals sleeping 10 guests for as low as $750-$1200 per week. Sharing costs with family and friends offers significant savings on luxury properties.

12| Caribbean Carnivals and Celebrations

Festivals and celebrations are a passion and priority in the Caribbean. Each year the calendar is filled with festivals, carnivals and celebrations around the region. Here's a sampling of annual parties in paradise:

- Antigua, Aruba, Curacao, the Cayman islands, Dominican Republic, Jamaica, St. Kitts and Nevis all celebrate annual **Carnivals or Carnavals** usually in the weeks preceding Lent.
- Jamaica is known as the home of reggae music and the **Reggae Sumfest** and **Air Jamaica Jazz and Blues Festival** are annual music festivals worth the trip.
- Learn to dance the Merengue at the **Santo Domingo Merengue Festival** .
- The **Barbados Jazz Festival** and **Puerto Rico Heineken Jazzfest** grow in popularity every year.
- St. Lucia lays claim to **"The Best Party in the Caribbean"** with a springtime jazz festival.
- June brings the **Goombay Festival** and in December you can celebrate the Christmas holidays with **Junkanoo** in the Bahamas.

If you enjoy a good celebration, plan ahead. Caribbean vacation rentals go fast around festival dates. Unlike most major holidays, these festival and celebration dates change each year and it is best to do an Internet search or check with the Island Tourism Authority for the current festival dates.

13| Caribbean Island Hot Spots

The islands of the Caribbean are filled with unique attractions and rich cultures. Here is a sample of what some popular Caribbean "hot spots" are known for:

- Caribbean includes the **U.S. Virgin Islands of St. Thomas, St. John and St. Croix.** If shopping and nightlife are your passion, St. Thomas offers some of the best shopping, best golf courses and most exciting nightlife in the Caribbean. It is also a popular cruise port with ships arriving early morning and sailing late in the afternoon. For a more secluded getaway and great snorkeling, opt for tiny St. John or St. Croix.
- Best windsurfing and kite boarding is found on **Barbados, Bonaire, Dominican Republic and Aruba.**
- **St. Lucia, St. Martin (French side), St. John and Peter Island** are most often cited as the "Most Romantic Caribbean Islands."
- **Anguilla, Bonaire, Nevis and Paradise Island, Bahamas** rank high on family-friendly lists.
- **St. Thomas, Puerto Rico, Jamaica, Aruba** and the **Dominican Republic** get top the leader board for great golfing.
- **Anguilla, Antigua, Aruba, Grand Cayman and Barbados** offer some of the most scenic beaches.
- **Grand Cayman Island** is a diver's dream with over 250 dive and snorkel sites and **Bermuda, Bonaire and Curacao** also offer great dive sites.
- *National Geographic* cites **Grand Cayman, Saba, Dominica and Montserrat** as the most extreme Caribbean landscapes.

14| Caribbean Shopping Savvy

Few travelers resist the lure of Caribbean shops, bazaars and markets. Research guidebooks and Websites and learn about local specialties. Make a list of things you want to buy and a gift list. Customs regulations and fees vary according to your destination. Read ***Know Before You Go*** from U.S. Customs to avoid having purchases confiscated or paying exorbitant duty fees. No matter where you shop, seek out unique mementos that have meaning long after your trip:

- **U.S. Virgin Islands** – Flavored rums and rum candy, fine jewelry, diver's watches and local crafts.
- **Bahamas** – Baskets, Rum and local crafts.
- **Antigua** – Duty-free Scottish cashmere, hand-printed fabrics, rum liquors, and silk robes and skirts.
- **Barbados** – English china, African-batik, spices, run, pottery, baskets and leather goods.
- **Cayman Islands** – Duty –free designer jewelry and perfume. Treasure-coin pendants and rings, chocolates, Caymanite beads, turtle sculptures and enamel iguanas.
- **Jamaica** – Appleton Rum, Tia Maria, Blue Mountain Coffee, Reggae CDs, knit caps and folk paintings.

- **Aruba** – Imported china and designer fashions. Aruba Aloe lotions, Delft blue tiles and vases, Palmera rum and coconut bonbons.
- **Grenada** – Spices and local crafts.

If you enjoy shopping in markets and bazaars, learn to bargain with best. Ask your Caribbean vacation rental agent/owner about local bargaining protocol.

As a general rule, begin bargaining at 50% off the asking price and expect to settle for about 30%-40% off the seller's original price. Don't haggle over pennies. When negotiations reach that point, give in or walk away.

Note: Consider the economic conditions where you are and how much a few cents means in a poor economy.

15| Caribbean Vacation Rental Reminders

There are many advantages to renting private beach houses and villas. First, there's the space. A hotel room becomes more confining each day when the entire family shares one room and bath or even a small suite. Vacation villas offer multiple bedrooms and baths, spacious living and dining areas and private outdoor amenities such as tropical gardens and plunge pools. Then, there's the benefit of being able to dine in privacy and avoid paying exorbitant resort dining charges. It's simple and economical to hire a local chef or whip up fresh seafood dinners in your own fully-equipped kitchen. No reservations required. No long wait times.

There are thousands of private beachfront vacation rentals on the Internet. Renting the right place for a honeymoon or family retreat requires research and due diligence. Follow these tips from a vacation rental specialist to ensure rental success:

- Make a list of everything you require for the "perfect stay."
- Search and compare Caribbean vacation rentals on the Internet. Note exactly what is and is not included in the rental. Study photographs for details. Read fine print carefully for restrictions and cancellation policies.

- Call rental agents or owners and clarify any questions or with special requests.
- Ask for references from previous guests.
- Ask about availability of discounts for early booking, multiple nights or advance payment.
- Contact local Tourism Boards to verify offers and inquire about past guest complaints.
- Book early for the best rates and dates. Bahamas vacation rentals in popular destinations fill rapidly, especially during high season (December-April).
- Never pay cash for a vacation rental. Paying with a credit or charge card offers buyer protection in case of default or problems.

It's a beautiful day in the Caribbean. What are you waiting for?

16| Finding a Caribbean Vacation Rental

Imagine pristine beaches fringed by elegant swaying palms. The air is perfumed by tropical blooms. Sparkling turquoise waters are warm and clear as you float above colorful reefs and surrounded by dozens of exotic tropical fish. At sunset, Mother Nature paints a masterpiece across the sea as you sip a tall, cool rum drink and feast of the bounty of the sea. It must be paradise.

The Caribbean Islands extends 1,700 miles from Cuba in the west to Barbados in the East and from the coast of South America north to Bermuda. There are 30 major islands and hundreds of lesser-known and private islands. Each year over two million American visitors escape Jack Frost or the doldrums of daily life for a vacation in this vacation paradise. The key to a perfect Caribbean getaway is choosing the right place to stay and play.

Give some thought to your travel personality and priorities. Is nightlife important? Need family-friendly activities for all ages to fill the days with fun? Want top-rated golf on scenic links? Looking for action and adventure or seclusion to relax and rejuvenate?

Caribbean accommodations run the gamut with full-scale, all-inclusive resorts like Sandals and Beaches, upscale condominiums, luxurious beachfront vacation villas big enough for family and friends and secluded beach houses perfect for romance.

One of the charms of the Caribbean is its diversity. No two islands are exactly alike. Search Internet sites of major travel publications such as Fodor's, Frommer's, Travel & Leisure and Lonely Planet for island information. The U.S. Department of State also offers sound advice on Caribbean travel health and safety. No doubt, smart Internet searches of Caribbean vacations rentals will lead you to the destination of your dreams.

17| Get a Day Pass to All-Inclusive Resorts

Here's a little known Caribbean Island tip: You can enjoy Caribbean stays and save money away from the crowds in the privacy of beach houses or beach vacation villas and tap the perks of all-inclusive resorts *without* paying their hefty daily room rates. Here's how it works: Purchase a day pass that provides access to resort facilities, including dining and bars. For instance, at **Hedonism II** in **Negril, Jamaica**, you can purchase a day or night pass and, once on property; enjoy the resort just like a guest, including unlimited dining and bars. Day passes cover all facilities from 10 am until 6:30 pm for $65. Night passes are $75 per person and cover all amenities from 6:30 pm until the wee hours.

Other resorts offering day passes include: **Harbour Village Beach Club on Bonaire, Sugar Bay Club on St. Kitts, Ti Kaye Village on St. Lucia, Sandals and Grand Royal Antiguan Beach Resort on Antigua.** Day passes are often *not* advertised, but there's nothing to lose by contacting all-inclusive resorts at your destination and requesting a day pass. Reservations are usually required and passes are limited during peak holidays periods.

18| Important Passport Update

Although proposed passport requirements changed frequently in recent years, according to the Department of State, ***Western Hemisphere Travel Initiative (WHTI):***

- Beginning **January 23, 2007** , ALL persons, including U.S. citizens, traveling by **air** between the United States and Canada, Mexico, Central and South America, the **Caribbean, and Bermuda** will be required to present a valid passport, Air NEXUS card, or U.S. Coast Guard Merchant Mariner Document.
- As early as **January 1, 2008** , ALL persons, including U.S. citizens, traveling between the U.S. and Canada, Mexico, Central and South America, the **Caribbean, and Bermuda** by **land** or **sea** (including ferries), may be required to present a valid passport or other documents as determined by the Department of Homeland Security. While recent legislative changes permit a later deadline, the Departments of State and Homeland Security are working to meet all requirements as soon as possible. Ample advance notice will be provided to enable the public to obtain passports or passport cards for land/sea entries

Don't wait. As deadlines draw near, passport applications will increase dramatically and processing will be delayed. Even if these deadlines are extended, the Department of Homeland Security always recommends traveling with passport identification. So, if you want to be ready to snap up last-minute Caribbean travel deals, be prepared with a current passport in hand.

19| Protect Your Caribbean Travel Investment

When was the last time you knew in advance that you or traveling companions would get sick or that a storm would close the airport and stop all travel? Travel is expensive and it pays to spend a few dollars more to protect your travel investment. Research insurance you already have. Many seniors are unaware that Medicare does not provide coverage outside the United States, including the Caribbean. If your personal health insurance does cover you, call customer service or visit their Web site for out-of-area and international claims procedures.

According to U.S. Department of State health and safety information, medical care in much of the Caribbean is limited and medical evacuations cost $35,000 or more on average. It's critical to know what insurance protection you do and do not have. A comprehensive travel policy covers both medical and trip cancellation/interruption events. The cost of travel insurance varies with the coverage provided. Least expensive is not the only criteria you should use to select a policy. Policies are priced by type of coverage, length of trip, cost of trip, and sometimes travelers' ages. Average cost of comprehensive travel insurance is approximately $65.00 per $1000 of the trip cost. Compare travel insurance policy terms and rates at InsureMyTrip.com.

20| Tropical Hurricane Fears and Facts

Since the Caribbean lies inside the Atlantic hurricane track and the best off-season Caribbean vacation rental rates fall within hurricane season (May-November), some travelers hesitate to take advantage of travel savings during this period. The chance of a hurricane disrupting your travel plans is minimal and improved weather forecasting provides advance notice of potential storms. Nevertheless, it pays to keep an eye on advance weather forecasts and protect travel investments with travel insurance. Another option is to vacation in the most southern Caribbean destinations such as Aruba or Barbados that lie outside the hurricane paths especially during the peak storm periods from mid-August through early October.

21| Finding a European Vacation Rental

The Internet is filled with European vacation rental options. You can rent directly from the property owner or through an agency specializing in vacation rentals. Visit the Websites and study the available properties. Most rental agency Websites feature extensive property details, photographs and contact details. Create a file of holiday rentals that pique your interest. Make a list of questions and vacation rental must-haves. Contact the owner or rental agency for more information. A reputable vacation rental agency saves time and frustration.

Leading agencies require that vacation rentals meet agency standards and provide assurance that someone will be available to assist you with questions and problems. Some agencies handle vacation rentals and travel details; others link rental requests directly to the property owner for booking and travelers must handle their own travel details.

Compare offers, rental restrictions and cancellation policies from several vacation rental agencies before making a final booking decision. Of course, the ideal way to find a European vacation rental is a recommendation from an experienced traveler. If you don't know who to ask, extend your research to travel Websites featuring personal travel reviews and forums where you can ask other travelers for vacation rental recommendations and all about the pleasures and pitfalls of your destination.

22| European Holiday Rental Etiquette

One of the greatest benefits of travel is the opportunity to experience different cultures and lifestyles. No one likes to be stereotyped as a "Tacky Tourist." Yet, travelers who are polite, patient, and pleasant at home sometimes behave and dress in ways that are inappropriate and offensive in other cultures. Use these tips to pave the way for smooth international relations while staying in your holiday rental.

- While you research where to stay, eat and sightsee at your destination, include research on customs and cultural sensitivities.
- Travel with an open mind and an open heart. Don't expect things to be the way they are "at home." Embrace the differences and learn from them.
- Everything is rarely perfect…at home or abroad. When problems crop up, keep your cool and sense of humor. Tact and diplomacy trump sarcasm and superiority every time.
- Purchase a small phrase book and learn a few words and phrases in the language of your destination. Some examples of key words/phrases include: please, thank you, hello, goodbye, emergency, need help and Where is…?
- Remember that your European vacation rental host is not your servant or concierge. They may help solve problems with your holiday rental, but they are not tour guides or errand runners.
- Avoid discussing politics, other controversial topics or criticizing the country in conversation with your holiday rental host and local residents.

23| Germany Vacation Rentals

Germany offers travelers an intriguing mixture of old and new cultural attractions and lively festivals fortified by unforgettable foods, beers and wines. Germany vacation rentals fall into three diverse categories. Make yourself at home in the center of the action in an apartment or house in the cities like Berlin, Munich, Stuttgart or Frankfort. Or, escape city crowds to a large villa, magnificent castle or simple farm cottage the countryside. Germany is synonymous with Oktoberfest in Munich. Sample your share of over 5,000 beers accompanied by specialty sausages, Weiner schnitzel and decadent Black Forest Cake. Forget the calories. They are worth every bite! Not a beer lover?

Thirteen regions in Germany grow grapes for award-winning wines. You won't be thrown out of the party if you raise a toast with a good German wine. If you want to attend the biggest party of the year, plan ahead. Make your reservations for a Germany vacation rental at least a year in advance.

24| Getting Around On A European Vacation

In major cities like Rome, Paris, Zurich or Berlin, a rental car may be a hindrance more than a help. Local transportation is plentiful, cheap and safe. For instance, in Paris you are never more than 550 yards from a Metro station and riding the subway is a cultural experience. Entertainers step on trains with violins or accordions, perform, pass the hat and step off at the next stop. Throughout Europe, it is easy to book local tours or hire a private guide for sight-seeing. Double-decker, hop-on/hop-off tour buses also blanket major cities making it easy to check off the must-see sights on your travel list. On the other hand, when staying in a Europe vacation rental outside major cities for an extended period and exploring the countryside, a rental car becomes a necessity. Research international rentals, and driving requirements and conditions, before leaving for your destination. Most major U.S. car rental companies have international offices.

Autoeurope is also a reliable source for comparing international rental car rates and terms. Unless your credit card company provides car rental coverage, you will need to purchase insurance. Check with American Automobile Association (AAA) before leaving the United States to apply for an **International Driver's Permit (IDP).** The IDP is a translation of your driver's license and is required by law in many European countries. Finally, pack your most comfortable walking shoes. European cities and villages are made for walking. It is great exercise and the best way to get to know and appreciate your destination.

25| Italy Vacation Rentals

Unpack and settle into an Italy vacation rental; the perfect base to explore this warm and friendly country by rental car or train. Holiday rentals run the gamut from simple and rustic to grand and luxurious. There are no-frills one-bedroom apartments at $500 per week, grand ten-bedroom villas in Tuscany for $5000 or more per week and everything in-between. Stay as long as possible because from the mountains to the rugged coastline there are many wonderful sights and activities you won't want to miss.

Skiers are attracted to the Aosta Valley with the most mountains in Italy. Milan is the fashion and automotive center. Rekindle romance with a gondola ride in Venice, explore the maritime heritage or spend an afternoon sipping chilled Prosecco and people-watching in Piazza of San Marco. Snap a photo at The Leaning Tower of Pisa in the Tuscany region and continue on to Florence, the capital of Tuscany. Don't miss the Uffizi Gallery, one of the world's most famous museums. On to Rome to make a wish at Trevi Fountain, stand in awe at Vatican City and hear the echoes of history at The Coliseum. Heading south, feel the chill of seeing Mt. Vesuvius towering over innocently over the ruins of Pompeii. Celebrate a day in Naples and hop over to Sicily for a close-up view of Mt. Etna. One visit to Italy is never enough. Instead of saying "arriverderci," you will be planning a return visit even as you wing your way home.

26| Making the Most of Your European Vacation Rental

One of the greatest pleasures of vacations rentals is the opportunity to get to know the country you are visiting and build relationships with the people. Unlike a quick getaway, you are staying a while. Make the most of your time by immersing yourself in the flavor of your destination. Do the must-see and must-dos on your travel list. Then, slow down and spend some time off the beaten path. There are many special travel moments that will stay in your heart and mind long after monuments and museums merge and blur.

- Relax at a sidewalk café and watch the world go by.
- Savor a sunset or sunrise.
- Talk to locals and learn what they like best about their world. Be open to spontaneous experiences and serendipity.
- Take new knowledge home with you. Attend local festivals, exhibits, performances or lectures at a local university. Book a language, cooking or pottery class. Each time you practice your new skill, you'll remember where you learned it.

- Spend an afternoon with the vintner at a local winery on your Italy vacation rental.
- Sign-up for ski lessons or discover how Swiss watches are made on your Switzerland vacation rental.
- Learn the art of making specialty sausages on your Germany vacation rental.

The Internet is filled with opportunities for unique experiences around the world. A travel journal is the best souvenir of your European vacation rental experience. Memories fade quickly. Writing a travel journal allows you to retrace, relive and share your journey for years to come.

Keep your journal and pen close at hand. Record interesting facts and resources. Capture impressions and emotions of the world around you. Write about interesting people you encounter. Your travel journal could become a travel book!

27| Questions to Ask About Holiday Rentals

Travelers in North America take for granted that accommodations come with every possible modern convenience. When staying in vacation rentals Europe it pays to ask questions to avoid disappointment. Here are a few important questions to ask your host *before* you book:

- **What comes with the holiday rental?** Most vacation rentals are equipped with linens and basic kitchen gear like dishes, flatware, pots and pans. Dishwashers and microwaves are rare except in luxury villas and inner city modern apartments. And, household staples and supplies (including toilet paper) are often not provided. Be prepared to make a quick shopping list and head for the market on arrival or ask if supplies can be pre-stocked for a fee.
- **Is there air conditioning/central heating/fireplaces?** Many European vacation rentals, especially in the countryside, have no air conditioning. Except in the height of summer, this is not a problem. Thick stone walls of villas and cottages and country breezes keep the in-door climate pleasant
- **Is there telephone/television/Internet access?** In the city, Internet Cafes are plentiful. Vacation rental telephones are scarce, especially outside the city. Consider renting or purchasing an international cell phone to stay in touch. Some rentals have satellite TV, but TV junkies may have to find other sources of entertainment.

- **When were photographs and amenities listed on the Website last updated?** If the listing is years old, furnishings may be shabby and conveniences may be outdated.
- **How far away are local markets/stores?** A morning stroll to the local village marketplace is an entertaining and educational part of the European holiday rental experience.
- **Is there a 24-hour English-speaking contact in the event of an emergency?** Know where to call if a pipe bursts or a toothache or tummy ache strikes in the middle of the night. (Check your health insurance or travel insurance policy for claims procedures and assistance abroad.)

Don't *assume* anything about a vacation rental at home or abroad. Read the fine print on rental contracts before booking. Ask questions and take abundant notes!

28| Switzerland Vacation Rentals

Switzerland vacation rentals offer a large selection of meticulously clean, comfortable and charming holiday rentals in incredibly scenic locations. Imagine majestic snow-capped mountains towering over crystal clear lakes. Choose from cozy studios, charming chalets, ski lodges and grand villas. A Switzerland vacation rental is the perfect base for exploring the sights in cities like Bern, Interlaken, Luzerne, Zurich and Geneva. Allow time to enjoy the friendly folks and outdoors in villages with intriguing names like Meiringen, Grindelwald and Lauterbrunnen. Picture a spacious Swiss Ski Lodge, one hour from Zurich by train, perched on slopes with stunning views of the Alps.

There are endless activities by day and by night. Snow bars and ski huts create a relaxed and sociable atmosphere. The main Lodge (sleeping 6-8 guests) consists of three bedrooms, a large bathroom, fully-equipped kitchen, central heating, TV, wireless Internet and plenty of amenities. High season rental rates of the range from $265-$325 per night. Off-season rates are as low as $135 per night and guests enjoy summer hiking, biking, swimming, windsurfing and shopping. Tempted? Plan ahead. Most Switzerland vacation rentals are booked six months in advance.

29| The Basics of European Vacation Rentals

In the United States, vacation rentals typically refer to vacation homes or condominiums in major cities or resort areas. In Europe, vacation rentals are referred to (in English) as self-catering rentals, holidays rentals, holidays villas and holiday cottages or chalets. They are found in the cities and the countryside, often on working farms or vineyards. There are many advantages to staying in a holiday rental.

Most European holiday rentals are for one week, a leisurely stay that allows you to get to "know" the country. Your vacation rental apartment or villa becomes a home base for exploring the countryside by rental car or train. Hotel rooms throughout most of Europe tend to be small. A vacation rental villa or apartment offers space and privacy.

Picture preparing your own picnic lunch or visiting the local markets, preparing dinner and dining al fresco the villa's vineyard or garden. Some up-scale properties come with the services of a chef or butler or you may want to include a cook or housekeeper in your travel budget. What a luxury!

On the flip side, European vacation rentals are not for everyone. Except for the most luxurious estates frequented by the rich and famous, there is more work to do. Less pampering. No daily maid service. No midnight room service.

Unless you are comfortable driving a rental car or there is local train or bus transportation, countryside vacation rentals may be far from must-see city sights and nightlife. Although vacation rentals typically cost less per day than a hotel, most require 50% of the rental at the time of the booking and the full amount of the rental a month or more before arrival. If you must cancel, refunds are rare. (Protect your investment with travel insurance!)

Finally, some travelers are intimidated by the logistics of vacation rentals and fear "making a mistake." It pays to do your homework when it comes to finding and choosing the best vacation rental for your personal priorities.

30| When to Book a Holiday Rental

If possible, plan your European vacation travel based on seasonal weather and seasonal rates. Summer throughout much of southern Europe is sweltering. Destinations are crowded and holiday rental rates are the highest. Winters, particularly in northern Europe, can be harsh limiting outdoor activities. Avoid travel during the high season when vacation rental rates are highest. This doesn't mean only traveling to Italy in sweltering August or Germany in frigid January. Plan your European vacation rental for the cusp or shoulder season; just before or right after high season.

Ask the vacation rental agency or owner when seasonal rates change. Although most Europeans book their vacations rentals a year ahead and often return to the same location each year, if your travel dates are flexible, look for last-minute vacation rental offers with savings of 30% or more. With the advent of the Euro, exchange rates have made vacation rentals in much of Europe more expensive. Countries currently using the Euro include the 12 members of the European Union: Austria, Belgium, Finland, France, Germany, Greece, Ireland, Italy, Luxembourg, The Netherlands, Portugal and Spain. However, there are ways to save money on holiday rentals even in these countries. In general, most frequent travelers agree that May and June, September and October are optimal travel months throughout most of Europe weather-wise and budget-wise.

31| Florida Vacation Overview

Florida claims the title of leading tourism state in the United States with good reason. Juan Ponce de Leon first landed in Florida in 1513 in search of the fabled Fountain of Youth. Although he never found the fountain, over 80 million visitors still flock to Florida from around the world year in search of fun and sun. The Florida peninsula boasts over 1200 miles of coastline framed by sparkling waters of the Atlantic Ocean and Gulf of Mexico.

If you walked one mile of Florida beach every day, it would take you over two-and-a-half years to get around the whole state. From the tip of the Florida Keys to central Florida's amazing theme parks to the scenic beaches of Florida's Emerald Coast in the most northwestern part of the state, Florida boasts more vacation home rentals than any other state. The most difficult part of planning a vacation to Florida is deciding where to stay and play.

32| Best Time to Visit Florida

Florida is a year-round vacation destination. However, consider these facts about when to get the best deals on Florida vacation rentals:

- South Florida high season rates are from mid-December through mid-March when winter wreaks havoc in the northeast. Summer in south Florida at hot and humid.
- North Florida experiences a change of seasons and opposite high seasons. Summer is high season. Fall and spring are optimal times to visit. Temperature on winter nights may occasionally drop near freezing and daytime temperature average 62 F.
- In the Orlando area, Disney theme parks are packed during summer months and holidays when the kids are out of school. If travel plans are flexible, take the kids out of school a few days and reserve your Disney home rental or Florida vacation rental during the shoulder season prior to or immediately after high season rates. For example, visit Disney in October, avoid crowds and enjoy the wonderful respite from summer heat and humidity.

After four major hurricanes hit Florida in 2004, many visitors expressed concerns about travel to Florida during hurricane season. Fortunately, major hurricanes are still a rare weather event. Florida has averaged only one major hurricane hit every two years in more than 100 years.

Nevertheless, hurricane season runs from June through November with the highest probabilities of a hurricane impact in mid-August through early October. Even if a tropical system is forecast for Florida, the storm can affect one part of the state while the sun shines in other parts. Early and improved weather forecasting also provides advance warning of potential weather problems.

If hurricanes are a concern, plan your Florida vacation rental for months outside of the seasons or protect your travel investment with travel insurance.

33| Blast Off on Florida's Space Coast

Florida's Space Coast runs along the east coast from Ormond Beach to Vero Beach in the south. Home to NASA and the Kennedy Space Center Visitor Complex; visitors get a firsthand look at America's exploration into space through interactive exhibits, movies and tours. Time your visit right and experience the thrill of watching a space launch. Check NASA's calendar for upcoming launch dates. A vacation rental home on the Space Coast is the perfect base for exploring the coast and central Florida attractions.

Less than one hour from Orlando, it is a short drive to Disney theme parks and other central Florida attractions. Nearby, Daytona Beach, often called the world's most famous beach, is 23 miles long and 500 feet wide at low tide. Daytona Beach draws race fans to the Daytona International Speedway and Daytona USA. Each year thousands of motorcyclists roll into town for Bike Week. There's always something exciting happening on Florida's Space Coast.

34| Emerald Coast Is a Florida Jewel

Florida's Emerald Coast runs along the panhandle of Florida from Pensacola to Panama City with over 100 miles of beaches. The sand is warm beneath your toes and sunlight sparkles like diamonds across emerald green Gulf of Mexico waters. Combine scenic shores with non-stop activities and it's easy to see why this part of Florida is consistently voted "Best Beach in the South" and "Top Family Destination" in nationwide polls each year.

Although the pristine, sugar-white sand beaches are the main draw, there's plenty to do off the beaches. Military buffs enjoy Pensacola's National Museum of Naval Aviation and the Air Force Armament Museum in Fort Walton Beach. Destin, "the world's luckiest fishing village," is home to the largest saltwater charter boat fleet in Florida. And, along the coasts of Okaloosa, Walton and Bay Counties golfers can play 18 holes of golf every day for over a month without playing the same hole twice.

A beach home rental offers the opportunity to have second home at the beach for a weekend, a week, a month or more and vacation rentals are a bargain on the Emerald Coast. Rent an upscale New England style cottage for two or ten at scenic Seaside or Rosemary Beach.

Check into a gulf-front condominium on Okaloosa Island in Fort Walton Beach and watch the dolphins play in the surf from your private balcony. Unlike South Florida where the winter is the high season, summer is the high season in northwest Florida.

Fall and spring months are considered the shoulder season and vacation rental rates plummet. Summer tourists are gone and temperate days are perfect on un-crowded beaches. Celebrate Thanksgiving in a three bedroom/three bath gulf-front luxury condominium that rents for $2,600 per *week* in the summer time, but is a bargain with off-season rates of $1600 or less per *month*.

35| Central Florida Is the Gateway to Family Fun

Walt Disney World in Orlando continues to lure more visitors than any other single attraction anywhere in the world. Multiple theme parks are packed with over 100 major attractions, including the Magic Kingdom, Epcot, Disney-MGM, Animal Kingdom, Blizzard Beach Water Park , Downtown Disney Marketplace and Pleasure Island . Universal Orlando, SeaWorld and Old Town-Kissimmee are other top entertainment venues. Deciding where to stay is a smart start. With over 25,000 hotel rooms, there's no shortage of places to stay in Orlando. However, one of the best kept secrets for a perfect stay is a Disney vacation rental.

After a tiring day at theme parks, don't return to a crowded hotel with an extra roll-away cot for the kids. Picture a spacious, fully-equipped Disney rental home with three or four bedrooms and three baths after a long day of touring the different parks. No waiting in line for the bathroom. Unwind with a tall cool drink by your private swimming pool. Later, grill burgers or steaks on the patio and feed the family for a few dollars rather standing in line at a crowded restaurant and dropping a small fortune. Frequent travelers estimate the average savings for a family of four staying in a Disney rental home at over $1,500 for one week.

36| Make the Most of Your Disney Vacation

The sheer number of vacation attractions and activities in the Orlando area are overwhelming. It pays to plan ahead to make the most of precious vacation time and dollars.

- Purchase the All-in-One-Hopper Pass and save admission costs for multiple Disney theme parks. A typical one day admission to one park is around $63 for ages 10+. A five-day Hopper Pass is $179 per person with advance purchase. (Purchase online through Disney for extra savings and benefits. The multiple admission/multiple day pass saves money and stress.)
- Don't try to "do it all in a day" at any theme park. Mix and match. Alternate tiring theme park activities with more passive pursuits. Come and go you please.
- Spend some of the dollars saved on your vacation rental stay for a Disney FASTPASS and avoid long waits for the most popular rides.
- No matter how well you plan, you can never see it all on one vacation to Central Florida.

A Florida vacation rental makes a memorable annual family tradition.

37| Life is Laid-Back in the Florida Keys

The Florida Keys sprawl 110 miles southwest of Miami, connected to the mainland by the causeways and bridges. Life in the Keys moves a little slower. Expect fun and funky; entertaining and eccentric. Travel temptations in the Florida Keys include:

- **Key Largo,** the first island from Miami, is a perfect escape from the doldrums of the real world. Spend seven days in a beach cottage complete with a sailboat, glass-bottom boat a kayak for lazy days on water or diving and snorkeling over shipwrecks at nearby John Penekamp State Park. Ahhh!
- **Islamorada** offers world-class off-shore fishing or try your hand at the art of bonefishing in shallow waters close to shore. Picture a barefoot four-bedroom vacation rental villa right on the beach just steps from crystal waters with room for eight friends and family.
- **Marathon Key** is the mid-way point in the Keys. A beachfront rental is the perfect base for exploring all the attractions in the Key archipelago.
- **Key West** is the southernmost point in the continental United States. Rent a tropical cottage or a penthouse condo right on the ocean. Laze away the days. Watch for the famous "green flash" sunset in Mallory Square, sample the hot nightlife on famous Duval Street. Beware! Life in the Florida Keys is contagious; a visit may turn into a lifetime.

38| Relax and Revive on Florida's Nature Coast

The west coast of Florida boasts miles of some of the top-rated beaches. The Sarasota, Bradenton, Tampa, St. Petersburg and Clearwater areas are home to Fort De Soto Park, America's No. 1-rated beach; Caladesi Island, America's No. 4-rated beach and Clearwater Beach, ranked No. 1 for city beaches on the Gulf of Mexico. Off the beach, more than 50 golf courses challenge the skills of beginners to pro golfers. From the Greek influence in Tarpon Springs to the Scottish heritage of Dunedin, 26 diverse communities offer cultural experiences for all tastes.

Florida vacation rentals on the west coast include charming beach cottages, elegant beachfront homes, beach compounds and condominiums. Choose a cozy Old-Florida style cottage for a romantic weekend getaway or bring the whole family and a dozen close to your own private beach compound. Accommodations include: six bedrooms, four baths, three kitchens, four living area, several decks and a two-story children's playhouse with a jungle gym. This great vacation rental home is only 50 steps from the beach. Rent this luxury private beach compound for $3,600 per week. Share the rent among four couples and it's a bargain at under $130 per couple per day.

Forget the expensive rental car. Tampa International Airport is 30 minutes away and the limo drops you at the door. Great seafood restaurant and a full marina are within two blocks.

39| South Florida Is Hot, Hot, Hot

Stroll the sidewalks of Miami's trendy South Beach. Soak up the sun on the beach by day and chill out with hot nightlife when the sun goes down. Introduce the kids to the Mother Nature's wonders in Everglades National Park. Hop aboard a day cruise for a taste of the Caribbean. Talk to the precocious primates at Monkey Jungle or the sea life at the Miami Seaquarium. South Florida is also home to other glamorous vacation destinations like Naples and Marco Island to the west and Ft. Lauderdale, Hollywood, West Palm Beach and Boca Raton on the east coast.

Vacation rentals range from a cozy beachfront rental studio tucked between multi-million dollar high-rise hotels on right on Miami Beach to a six luxury bedroom home rental sleeping 12 guests. In-season rates run from $600 to $6000 per week. Save 30%-50% with off season rates

40| Where to Stay and Play in Florida

Florida is all about diversity when it comes to attractions, activities and accommodations. Let your personal interests determine your location. Florida is a golf Mecca; lauded as the golf capital of the world. Florida is the first choice for avid anglers. In addition to off-shore saltwater fishing expeditions, there are nearly 30,000 lakes and rivers for fresh water fishing. Florida is an affordable, family-friendly destination with the largest concentration of theme parks in the U.S. And, a trip to Florida also offers a bounty of rich ethnic experiences and historical treasures. If you have missed the pleasures of a Florida vacation rental, you've come to the right place for some great tips from visitors who return year after year to escape Old Man Winter in the "Sunshine State." If you dream of idyllic days relaxing on the beach, a seaside cottage, condominium or villa puts the beach on your doorstep.

When visiting major cities like Orlando, a centrally located Disney rental home near major theme parks offers convenience, cost-saving and a relaxing haven from cramped hotel rooms. Newlyweds or 50th anniversary honeymooners often seek romantic Florida vacation rentals away from busy tourist attractions. And, golfers throughout Florida book vacation rentals right on the greens.

41| Things to Consider in Planning a Golf Getaway

If golf is your game, golf vacation rentals will fit you to a tee. Some golfers dream of playing in the footprints of famous golfers like Tiger Woods on award-winning golf courses. Some golfers like to escape winter doldrums with a leisurely golf getaway in the tropics. For serious golfers, the more challenging a course, the better. Bring on the hazards, tricky shots and elements like wind, rain, sleet or even snow. Since golf personalities run the gamut, here are some initial questions to consider in matching a golf vacation to your personal preferences:

- What do you consider the "perfect" golf vacation? Serious golf, leisurely play or a mix-and-match of golf and non-golf activities?
- How long can you spend on your golf getaway? If time is limited to a few days, stay close to home and limit travel time.
- Do you want to play a different course each day? Choose a destination with multiple courses within a 30 minute drive.
- How healthy is your golf budget? Play at private courses is pricey. Look for public greens and discounts.
- Will you be bringing along the family or other non-golfers? Look for fun activities to fill the hours while you are on the greens.

With the answers to these questions in mind, continue on for some tips on making the most of any golf vacation.

42| Choosing a Golf Vacation Destination

Golf-a-holics recommend choosing a vacation destination based on how many courses are within easy access. A little research helps pick the best location for your games. Some good resources for researching golf opportunities are: Golf Digest, Golf & Travel, and Leisure Golf Magazine. Websites for golf organizations like United States Golf Association (USGA) and International Golf Federation (IGF) also provide golf destination inspiration. Of course, word of mouth is an important source for recommendations. Avid golfers love to talk about where they have played and share pleasure and pitfalls of golf destinations and courses. There is no shortage of worldwide golf destinations.

According to Mintel International Group, a Chicago market research firm, there are over 32,000 golf courses worldwide and more open every year. Internationally, according to Golf Digest (at the end of 2005), the countries with the most golf courses were: the United States, Scotland, New Zealand, Australia, Ireland, Canada, Wales, Sweden and England. The United States boasts over 17,000 courses and Florida tops the leader board with over 1,300 courses. Other leading U. S. golf destination states include: Arizona, California and Hawaii. Hilton Head and Myrtle Beach are also golf favorites. Where in the world do you want to play? Once you choose your dream golf destination, it's time to get serious about travel logistics.

43| Family Golf Vacations

Golf getaways and vacations offer wonderful bonding opportunities for the whole family. When you tee of with a tot or teen, you automatically have a leisurely sports experience with time for conversation away from demanding jobs and hectic school activities. Involve the family in planning a golf vacation. Research family-friendly golf courses, golf schools and golf clinics before you book your golf vacation.

The Family Golf Association (FGA) is dedicated to promoting golf as a family activity. For instance, FGA-member courses eliminate greens fees and cart fees for juniors when they're accompanied by a paying adult, establish family tee times and family guest fees. Golf vacation rentals offer many advantages for a family stay and play vacation. After days together on the links, you don't have to return to a night in a cramped hotel room. With a three or four bed villa or vacation home, everyone has their own bedroom and privacy to rest up for tomorrow's rounds. No waiting for the bathroom. The kitchen is always open for a midnight snack. Relaxing in the swimming pool while Dad grills burgers beats standing in line for restaurant reservations.

A quick online search for "family friendly golf courses" and "family golf clinics" turns up great family golf getaway destinations around the world. For instance, the Orlando and Kissimmee area abound with family-friendly golf vacation rentals and it's easy to combine green time and Disney theme park visits.

44| Golf Getaways for the Girls

Once upon a time golf was a guy's game…a traditional male domain. Move over guys; times have changed. According to Sven Kessler, VP of Retail Sales for Edwin Watts Golf, the largest privately-held golf company in the world, "Four out of every 10 new golfers are women."

The Champions Course, designed by Rees Jones, in Daytona Beach was the first golf course in history designed for professional women golfers and has been named "America's Best Women Friendly Golf Course." Throughout the world, there are golf courses that cater to women players and golf vacations are becoming a popular girlfriends' getaway. Couples golf is also becoming a norm rather than a rarity.

A typical "Golf Getaway for the Girls" goes like this: Four girlfriends leave the guys at home and escape for three nights in a luxury golf vacation rental home in northwest Atlanta. The gourmet kitchen is perfect for opening a couple of bottles of wine and sharing secrets while whipping up a delicious dinner. The next morning, a golf clinic hones putting skills followed by a round of golf at nearby Legacy Golf Course or Fox Creek. Day three is a morning of pampering at an Atlanta day spa followed by a champagne brunch and serious shopping Lenox Square and Phipps Plaza. There's also a star-studded night at the famous Fox Theater. Finally, the ladies end the weekend with a final round of golf. Find out more about women's golf schools, tournaments and play opportunities online at Play Golf America or the Ladies Professional Golf Association (LPGA).

45| Romantic Golf Getaways for Couples

Although romance is not usually the first thing that comes to mind when planning a golf getaway, perhaps it's time to think again. Re-kindle romance with a couple's golf getaway; playing and staying together in a romantic setting. If both partners golf, it's easy to mix tee times with other activities.

Here's a tempting sample: Spend a long weekend at a golf vacation rental in Cabo San Lucas. Casa Bella Condominiums combines luxurious and romantic beachfront living with world-class golf. Terrace views overlook the sparkling Sea of Cortez and the eighth hole of the famous Jack Nicklaus Ocean Course, ranked as one of the top 100 courses in the world. Resort management arranges tee times and discounts at other nearby championship golf courses. Follow a day of golf with a candlelight alfresco dinner for two caressed by warm sea breezes under a starry sky. And a few more ideas for golf and romance:

- If a partner is a non-golfer, be sure to include surprise treats, such as a day of pampering at a spa or shopping spree.
- Hire a personal chef for romantic in-suite, pool-side or on the beach.
- Surprise your partner with theater tickets and a dinner for two at the most romantic restaurant in town.
- Re-new your wedding vows on scenic links at sunrise or sunset.
- Putt and propose on the 18th hole followed by a private champagne celebration. Who says golf isn't romantic?

46| Golf Vacation Rentals Are a Smart Choice

Golf vacation packages are endless online and through travel providers and resorts. Typical packages include: accommodations based on double occupancy and one round of play on specified courses each day. While golf package prices may seem competitive, there is little flexibility. If deviations are allowed they add significant increases to the package price. Rather than restricting your options, golf vacation rentals offer the least expensive way to play with virtually unlimited play and stay options.

Picture this: Four golf buddies rent a beautiful golf vacation rental right on the greens. They hit the grocery and stock up on essentials for breakfast, sandwich making, grilling out and stocking the bar. A fully-stocked kitchen saves travel dollars that can be used for more rounds at more courses. A four bedroom villa offers the privacy of no shared bedrooms. Then, there's the camaraderie factor. Instead of sitting around a crowded bar, they gather around the pool to grill steaks and rehash the day. What a great way to go!

The same benefits apply to family vacation accommodations. Whether the golf vacation rental choice is a home or a condominium, no one has to share a bed. There's no waiting for the bathroom; no competition for a single TV. While Dad or Mom golf, the gang can go sightseeing, shopping or swim in their own swimming pool. Many vacation home rentals also offer game rooms and exercise rooms. Begin your search online. You're sure to find what you're looking for.

47| Book Tee Times Early

After settling on a destination and booking your golf vacation rental, it's time to score tee times. Don't wait until arrival at your destination and hope for the best. Tee times at most golf courses can be booked 90 to 180 days in advance. Call the courses you want to play and talk to the head pro. Friendly and appreciative trumps demanding when it comes to getting preferential treatment. Explain that your golf group will be vacationing nearby and that you look forward to playing one or more rounds on their course. Follow up with: "What can you do for us?" Booking online is also a good way to grab tee times at a discount. Do an Internet search using the name of the golf course. Discount play and tee times can also be booked through special golf booking Internet sites. Begin your search with the phrase "online golf tee times and discounts" for dozens of booking resources.

Tip: Confirm all tee times booked online or by telephone a few days prior to play.

48| Save Money on Golf Getaways

There's a common perception that "golf is not a poor man's game." True, a round of golf can easily cost several hundred dollars at a private club. Unlike purchasing a soccer ball or baseball bat, Golf clubs and accessories are expensive. However, there are ways to save money on a golf vacation:

- Choose a golf vacation rental rather than a resort. Vacation home rentals almost always work out to less per day than a golf resort hotel. Combine accommodation costs with the benefits of full-equipped kitchen and outdoor grilling and save more dollars on dining.
- Book your getaway for the shoulder or off-season at your golf destination. Vacation rental rates average 30% less off-season. Golf courses are not as busy and most offer reduced green fees.
- The **Golf Digest Passbook** membership card is a premier golf savings program offering 20-50% discounts at 2,500 courses, learning centers, golf tournaments and on golf products. Regional golf publications often have discounted or two-for-one coupons. Finally, check directly with local courses for special early morning or weekday discounts.

49| Think Location, Location, Location

Real estate professionals say the three most important words are "location, location, location." The same three words apply to a golf vacation rentals. Another advantage of a golf vacation rental is the ability to choose a convenient location for your stay. A hotel or resort golf package is usually based on playing on-site greens. Other area courses may be an hour or more away. When staying at a golf destination with multiple courses, save travel time between courses by choosing a golf vacation home in a central location. For instance, there are over 350 golf courses in Arizona and over half of these courses are in the Phoenix-Scottsdale area.

Choose a centrally located vacation home for a week's vacation and it's easy to play a different course every day or one course in the morning and another in the afternoon without traveling great distances. There are also plenty of entertainment options for non-golfers and after-golf hours.

50| Traveling with Your Golf Gear

Most golfers prefer to play with their own golf clubs. However, a group traveling to a golf vacation rental with full golf gear may pose problems. Clubs are bulky and heavy and they may exceed airline weight limits and incur over-weight baggage fees. Even on a driving vacation, four golfers traveling by car with four sets of clubs requires a van or large SUV. Use these tips to facilitate traveling with your golf gear:

- Protect clubs with a study golf bag and purchase a shipping box to prevent possible damage to your golf bag through baggage handling.
- Conserve space by storing all your golf accessories in your golf bag.
- Consider shipping your golf gear ahead of time to your destination.
- Don't assume your golf gear is covered by your homeowner's insurance. Check your policy coverage and deductibles. If your clubs are top-of-the-line expensive, you may need to take out an additional policy endorsement (rider) covering loss or damage.
- Keep all sales receipts for your golf bag, clubs and accessories. If gear is lost, the airlines or your insurance company will require proof of value and replacement is subject to limitations.
- At your destination, always store golf gear inside your golf vacation rental rather than leaving gear subject to easy theft in the car overnight.
- Consider bringing limited golf gear, such as your favorite putter, and renting additional gear.

51| Choosing Your Hawaii Island

When it's time to run away to a Hawaii vacation rental, the first step is to decide which island or islands you want to visit. The big eight islands include: Oahu , Maui , Hawaii (the Big Island), Kauai , Molokai , Lanai , Niihau and Kahoolawe. (Note: Kahoolawe is unpopulated and Niihau is privately owned. Neither island is open to the public.) Here are some questions to help you decide which island matches your personal vacation preferences:

1. **Do you enjoy non-stop attractions and activities**? An Oahu vacation rental offers the most entertainment, sightseeing activities and nightlife…and crowds.
2. **Do you enjoy outdoor fun**? Maui is a Mecca for outdoor adventure…above and below the water and high in the mountains. Snorkel or dive in crystal waters. Hike or bike down a volcano. Play tag beneath a waterfall. Golf scenic and challenging greens. Don't miss sunrise over the Haleakala Crater.
3. **Want to relax and revive?** Kauai vacation rentals are havens of serenity away from the crowds on larger islands.
4. **Bringing the kids?** Choose a Waikiki vacation rental for loads of activities for all ages or a Maui vacation for outdoor fun.

52| Facts You Should Know About Hawaii

Here's some trivia to pique your interest in a Hawaii vacation rental:

- Hawaii is not a single place. There are eight main islands and over 100 islets (tiny uninhabited islands) sprawling in a crescent shape across 1,500 miles in the Pacific Ocean.
- If you want get away as far away from the rest of the world as possible, the Hawaiian Islands, located 2390 miles from California, 3,850 miles from Japan and 5,280 miles from the Philippines, is the most isolated inhabited island in the world.
- The Hawaiian word "Aloha" is both a greeting and a farewell and it means love. No doubt, you will fall in love with Hawaii and bid farewell only until you can return again and again to this sparkling Pacific paradise.

53| Visiting More Than One Island

There's an unwritten rule in the Hawaiian Islands. Don't try to see all the islands in one trip unless you are staying a month or more. Most frequent visitors recommend booking your vacation rental on Oahu, Maui, the Big Island or Kauai and making it your base for explorations. Budget at least five days to enjoy your island base. You still won't get to see it all and do it all, but it's a good start.

Avoid scheduling every hour of the day and night. Slow down and savor the Hawaiian experience. Then, branch out with an inter-island cruise or day trip to smaller islands like Molokai and Lanai. Check out island sightseeing and outer island day trips with local tour companies. An online search of "inter-island day trips Hawaii" yields plenty of choices by sea and by air.

54| When It's Time For A Hawaii Vacation Rental

It's the height of winter. Snow covers your rooftop. You need to shovel the sidewalk...again. It's time to trade that snowsuit for a tropical shirt and sip a tall, cool Mai Tai on a beach warmed by tropical breezes year-round. It's time to run away to Hawaii. It's a stressful commute in heavy traffic every day to a demanding job. You daydream of running away to a serene paradise. It's time to escape that stress and run away to Hawaii. You've always dreamed of saying "I Do" (or "I Still Do") in one of the most romantic spaces on earth. It's time to run away to Hawaii.

Family vacation time rolls away and as usual, no one can agree on where to go. The kids want to snorkel, surf and see the sights. Mom wants to relax and rejuvenate. Dad wants to get in a few rounds of world-class golf. It's time to run away to Hawaii. Your group of buddies craves adventure...hiking, biking, diving, surfing, exploring. It's time to run away to Hawaii.

55| Kauai is the Garden Isle

Don't come to Kauai for the nightlife unless you plan to make your own nightlife. Come for the incredible beauty and serenity surrounded by fragrant tropical flowers and foliage. Come for romance and the wonderful feeling of being alone together in your private paradise. Marvel at the grandeur Waimea Canyon and the rugged green cliffs of the Na Pali Coast. You'll quickly see why Kauai has been the location of movies like Jurassic Park, South Pacific and Blue Hawaii. Escape the real world in Kauai vacation rentals. Beachfront havens wait for you in a place where Hawaiian kings and high chiefs once sought solitude and artists and writers have found inspiration through the years. Beware: You may never want to leave this serene piece of paradise

56| Maui is the Valley Isle

It's no surprise that readers of *Conde Nast Traveler* have repeatedly named Maui the "Number One Island in the World". A favorite of honeymooners *and* families, Maui is an island of lush tropical rainforests, verdant valleys, volcanic mountains and golden sand beaches. Maui is also the best island for whale-watching. Each year humpback whales migrate to the waters off Maui. Between January and March, it is not uncommon to see more whales in the waters off Maui than on an Alaska cruise. A stay on Maui should include driving the famous Road to Hana, a beautiful 50-mile twisting and turning road through tropical scenery.

Take a break frequently and enjoy a swim under a waterfall. Hana is commonly known as the "Last Hawaiian Place." Step back in time with a Maui vacation rental plantation cottage in Hana. Honeymoon in a private studio suite in Lahaina Shores. Wake-up caressed by fragrant ocean breezes to the sound of gentle waves and tropical birds. Enjoy amazing sunsets and an evening luau on the beach and feel the humdrum world slip away.

57| Oahu is the Gathering Place

An Oahu vacation rental is a good home base for your Hawaiian getaway. Although there are direct flights from the mainland to each of the four biggest islands, there are more flights into Honolulu or Oahu than to any of the other islands. Consequently, there are more non-stop flights and airfare specials from major cities like Chicago, Atlanta, New York, San Francisco and Seattle. If you like being in the center of the action, Oahu is known as The Gathering Place. Choose a Waikiki vacation rental on the beach with views of Diamondhead.

Waikiki Beach is crowded, but offers great people-watching and Waikiki is a good place for beginners to learn to surf. Waikiki also offers the most nightlife in the islands. If you are looking for Oahu vacation rental options away from the action on Waikiki Beach, Sunset Beach and Waimea Bay are scenic surfing beaches. Imagine view from a beautiful four bedroom/three bath home on the famous North Shore of Oahu just a short walk to Waimea Bay Beach and Sharks Cove. Watch the surfing daredevils run gigantic breakers or opt for great swimming and snorkeling at Three Tables beach. Other popular Oahu vacation rental locations include: Turtle Bay, Ewa Beach, Kaaawa, Kailua and Lanikai.

58| The Big Island WOW Factor

On Hawaii, the Big Island, the WOW factor is high. It is the most ecologically diverse of the Hawaiian Islands. Two massive volcanoes create micro-climates with one side of the island hot and dry and the other side lush and tropical. Climb to the top of Mauna Kea for spectacular view, stay for the sunset and watch the sky fill with glittering starlight. Hawaii Volcanoes National Park is home of active volcanoes Kilauea and Madame Pele. Take a heart-stopping exciting helicopter and peer in the seething cauldron of Kilauea. It's the experience of a lifetime. Enjoy an afternoon on the unique Black Sand Beach of Punalu'u. Hawaii vacation rentals are as diverse as the island itself.

Choose a secluded cottage or condo on the beach or spread out on your own private 10-acre ranch with ocean and mountain views. Enjoy yourself in the own outdoor private pool, spa, tennis court overlooking the ocean or relax in your indoor dry/steam sauna. Watch the sunset over the Pacific and make a wish as the sky fills with glittering stars. This is life at its best.

59| Saving Money on a Hawaii Vacation Rental

Savvy research and careful planning offer savings throughout the islands. Peak travel times are based on weather and holidays on the mainland and in Asia. For instance, during Golden Week in Japan late April/early May, hoards of Japanese tourists come to Hawaii, especially Honolulu. Ironman Week in October fills the Big Island. Want to spend Christmas in Hawaii? Plan ahead. The demand for vacation rentals during the Christmas holidays is always high.

Dining out is expensive in Hawaii. Share meal and snack preparation in your fully-equipped kitchen and the savings add up fast. With the exception of Oahu, you need a rental car to explore the islands from your Hawaii vacation rental base. Rent a convertible and travel in style.

Fortunately, rental car rates in Hawaii are among the lowest in the country. Weekly rentals offer the best discounts. Check Into AAA and VIP car rental discount programs for more savings. Sightseeing excursions can take a bite out of any travel budget. Don't leave home without purchasing a Hawaii Gold Card for $30. Sold by the Activity and Attractions Association of Hawaii (a nonprofit trade association of over 200 activity and tour operators), the gold card looks like a credit card with your unique number imprinted on it. This number is all you need to book all types of activities at discounted prices. Plan your itinerary before you leave home and book popular attractions in advance. Take advantage of significant on every island on everything from rental cars and restaurants to luaus, water sports and helicopter rides. Aloha....until next time!

60| Where to Stay in the Islands

There are four primary types of lodging in the Hawaiian Islands. First, there are a limited number of bed and breakfasts found in the islands that run the gamut from simple to lavish. Major hotel brands offer budget priced to upscale properties on one or more islands with the largest hotel presence in Honolulu. Most large resorts are found on Oahu and Maui and rooms at resorts tend to cost more than hotels.

Note: Although travel agencies promote all-inclusive resort packages to Hawaii, these are *not* the same all-your-food-and-drinks all-inclusive deals popular in the Caribbean. These all-inclusive offers usually refer to a room, rental car and sometimes rounds of golf.

Live like the rich and famous in a Hawaii vacation rental estate perched above the blue Pacific on the Big Island. Every room offers panoramic views. A large solar-heated pool Jacuzzi, stone BBQ pit and expansive lanai offer plenty of space for entertaining, relaxing, sunning and star gazing. The main house features three bedrooms and baths and a detached, fully equipped apartment offers additional space. This estate easily tops $1 million dollars, but can "belong" to you and 5 or 6 guests for $440 per night (three-night minimum) or $2660 for a full week. Do the math. A comparable resort hotel room at $300 per night is $2100 per week. Three couples would spend over $6300 for a week in hotel rooms. Savings on accommodations alone: $4200.

Hawaiian vacation home and condominium rentals are rapidly becoming the most popular choice for Hawaiian holidays. Here are a few reasons why:

- **Space** : Why stay in a single cramped hotel room when you can have the run of an entire villa or condominium?
- **Privacy** : Togetherness is great, but too much togetherness adds stress and strain to any vacation. Why share beds and baths when everyone can have their own space?
- **Affordability:** On average Hawaiian vacation rentals cost 30% less than resort accommodations. When family and friends travel together and share the cost, a vacation rental offers ultimate luxury for less.
- **Flexibility** : Staying in a home, villa or condo provides the freedom to stay and play on your own schedule. Want a midnight snack? Raid the kitchen. Prepare your own meals or a picnic to enjoy by the pool or in a tropical garden setting. No waiting for restaurant reservations.
- **Luxury:** Not everyone can afford a luxury second home on a tropical island. Vacation rentals offer the chance to sample the rewards of luxury living without the risks of ownership.

61| A Taste of Lake Tahoe

They say there is no sight on earth like the first view of Lake Tahoe. Bordered by both Nevada and California, Lake Tahoe is unique. It is the highest alpine lake in the United States. It is also one of clearest, deep blue lakes in the world. Lake Tahoe's three trillion gallons of water is so clear that a 10-inch white dinner plate would be visible at 75 feet below the surface. No doubt, you will want to get a taste of Lake Tahoe by land, water and air during your Lake Tahoe Vacation rental. Although it is less than 100 miles around Lake Tahoe, driving can be hazardous in the winter and summer traffic can be frustrating, but in spring and early fall a drive around Lake Tahoe offers changing vistas on each shore.

By water, the M.S. Dixie II and Tahoe Queen are authentic paddlewheel cruises offering glass bottom viewing of the crystal clear waters, champagne brunches or dinner/dance cruises under the stars. By air, Balloons Over Lake Tahoe, Lake Tahoe Balloons and Mountain High Balloons offer the ultimate experience of soaring gracefully over meadows, mountains and skimming the blue waters of Lake Tahoe. Get a taste of Lake Tahoe and get ready for fun.

62| Plan Ahead for a Lake Tahoe Rental Vacation

Lake Tahoe is one of the hottest vacation destinations in the U.S., especially during ski season. Popular vacation rentals fill fast. Many visitors book a year in advance, reserving their favorite vacation home year after year.

When it comes to Lake Tahoe ski promotions and special event options, visit Ski Tahoe online early and often. Multi-ski ticket packages that are often sold out before the first snowfall. (The Six-Pack for six Ski Tahoe resorts sold out long before the 2006 season kicked off.) If you miss a seasonal promotion, take heart. There are numerous individual ski resort promotions on tickets, lessons and entertainment options. For instance, the Sierra-at-Tahoe's Family Pack Lesson Program is a great value for families wanting to learn together and have fun doing it. The full-day package includes a two-hour skiing or snowboarding lesson, equipment rental and beginner lift access for each family member. The Family Pack lesson is a private introduction lesson tailored specifically to the individual family and is available by advance appointment only. The cost for the 'learn to ski' or 'learn to snowboard' Family Pack is $240 for four family members. Or, use your American Express Card to receive 25% off an Intermediate or Advanced Performance Package, which includes an all-day lift ticket, performance rental equipment and a 1 hour 45 minute Mountain Adventure lesson.

Repeat this travel mantra; "Plan Ahead" and don't miss the deals, discounts and delights at Lake Tahoe.

63| Day Tripping Around Lake Tahoe

In the unlikely event that you have your fill of action on the slopes and in the casinos of Lake Tahoe, there are plenty of day trips to fill the gap.

- **Truck on over to Truckee**. The scenic 90-minute drive to Truckee winds through the Sierra Nevadas. The most scenic trip is Route 207 Kingsbury Grade, west on Highway 50 to Highway 28. Continue west, passing through Incline Village to California Route 267. Turn right on Route 267 and follow it to Truckee. Once in Truckee, the downtown area is a walking history lesson combined with contemporary specialty shops.
- **Go on a treasure hunt**. In summer and early fall (before snow covers the ground) is a great time to drive over to the Gold Hill/Virginia City area and scour the countryside for crystals and gem stones. Gold and silver streak through quartz and granite crystals. Large and small crystals are on the ground and tucked into nooks and crannies in the hills among bigger rocks. The best crystals are often found along the ditches on the road to Silver City, especially after a big rain when they get washed from the surrounding hills. (Heads up: Obey "No Trespassing" signs and watch out for rattlers on hot summer days!) Take your treasures back to your vacation home rental; they make great free souvenirs and gifts.

- **Take a hot bath**. Many years ago people believed that special curative powers existed in natural hot springs. Maybe so; maybe not. Regardless, a relaxing soak a perfect way to soak away aches and pains from exertion on the slopes or sooth the spirit after a long night at a casino. Rejuvenate with a soak at Grover Hot Springs State Park. From South Lake Tahoe it's a 35-minute drive through scenic Hope Valley, across the West Fork of the Carson River and east on U.S. Highway 88. Return to your vacation home renewed and ready for another night of fun.

64| Enjoy Lake Tahoe Special Events

With more than 400 events ranging from "Pray for Snow Parties" to quirky bashes, contests and festivals, there's always something going on in Lake Tahoe. Here's a short sample of annual events on the calendar at Lake Tahoe:

- The Annual May **Ski Nautique Gates & Wakes Fun Day and Pro Challenge** at Alpine Meadows combines skiing or snowboarding in the morning at Alpine Meadows and wakeboarding or water skiing on Lake Tahoe in the afternoon.
- **Elvis Day** is all about the King at Mt. Rose. Elvis is everywhere. He's lifting your ski ticket, fitting your skis and teaching ski lessons. Elvis entertains in local nightclubs and pubs. Skiers don their best Elvis look-a-like garb. Don't forget your camera for this hilarious event on the Saturday closest to the King's birthday January.
- On a cultural note, Lake Tahoe is home to the nationally recognized summer **Lake Tahoe Shakespeare Festival** at Sand Harbor State Park. For more than 25 years, visitors have spread out on the pristine beaches with wine and cheese, enjoying the Bard at his best.
- Audiences of all ages are delighted by the summer-long **Lake Tahoe Music Festival** . Each summer the festival offers a wide variety of programs, including classical, pops, Broadway, bluegrass, swing, blues, and jazz played in gorgeous, mostly outdoor locations around Lake Tahoe.

- The **American Century Celebrity Golf Championship Golf Tournament,** held in July each year at Edgewood Tahoe, is rated as one of Golf Digest's Top 25 public U.S. golf courses

Heads up: Check the calendar at Lake Tahoe Chambers of Commerce and Visitors Centers for a full list of special events. Plan ahead. Many visitors schedule their Lake Tahoe vacation rentals around favorite special events.

65| Family Fun in Lake Tahoe

For the family who enjoys the outdoors together, Lake Tahoe is a perfect choice for a family vacation rental any time of the year. There is so much going on you will never hear, "Mom...We're bored."

Most area ski resorts offer ski lessons for the kids and off the slope programs. For instance, full-day children's lessons at Heavenly for ages 4-13 cost $155 and include instruction, equipment, helmet, lunch and lift tickets.(Advance reservations are a must!) At **Rosebud**, the Children's Center is a one-stop center for families. Half-day group lessons start at $ for ages 4-13 and full day lessons are $130 including all ski gear, meals and lift tickets. Off the ski slopes, sample these activities for family fun:

- **Borges Family Sleigh Ride** and **Kirkwood Sleigh Ride** take families over the rivers and through the woods. Families enjoy snow play beyond the big resorts at North Tahoe Regional Park where a $5 fee includes a choice of a sled, tube or saucer.
- Schedule a family picnic at the lookout at **Vikingshol**, a reproduction of a Viking castle. Ride the Heavenly Gondola for breathtaking views any time of the year.
- Step back in history at the **Gatekeeper's Cabin Museum**. Let the kids try their hand at boat building, watercolors and other crafts at the Tahoe Maritime Museum.

After a day of fun, gather around the fireplace for old time games and story-telling. Lake Tahoe vacation rentals often become an annual family tradition.

66| Finding Lake Tahoe Vacation Rentals

When planning a visit to Lake Tahoe, it's important to understand the geography. Part of Lake Tahoe lies in California and part of it lies in Nevada. Locals refer to Tahoe geography by North and South shores. Some visitors prefer North Lake Tahoe vacation rentals; others prefer South Lake Tahoe vacation rentals.

If you are looking for entertainment and nightlife, head south to the Nevada side. Begin your vacation rental search online using search phrases like "south lake tahoe vacation rentals." You'll discover hundreds of choices ranging from romantic studios for two to a two-bedroom condo perched high above the lake or a luxury five-bedroom ski-in, ski-out chalet. If you aren't there to ski, save 40% or more off-season in late spring, summer and early fall.

For outdoor activities, think north. Using a search phrase "north lake tahoe vacation rentals," you'll be delighted with vacation rental choices ranging from rustic log cabins to luxurious chateaus sleeping you and 10 or so close friends. Regardless of which side you choose, there is no shortage of vacation home rentals and no shortage of fun in the Lake Tahoe area.

67| Getting To and Around Lake Tahoe

Once you have booked your vacation home rental, it's time to plan travel logistics. Traveling by air to Lake Tahoe, most visitors fly into the Reno/Tahoe, Sacramento, San Francisco, San Jose or Oakland airports. Reno-Tahoe Airport is just 45 miles from Lake Tahoe and offers over 170 flights with major airlines. Sacramento is 90 miles to the west and San Francisco is 200 miles away. In summer, it's a pleasant drive from Sacramento or San Francisco, but be sure to check Lake Tahoe weather and road conditions when driving during winter months. Most national rental car companies offer car rentals at the Reno/Tahoe International Airport.

If you want to take full advantage of seeing Lake Tahoe and interesting day trips, you will find a rental car helpful. If you are in Lake Tahoe for the action on the slopes during ski season and are not accustomed to driving in hazardous winter road conditions, opt for local transportation and choose a vacation home rental in the center of the action. South Tahoe Express offers transportation between Reno/Tahoe International Airport and South Lake Tahoe Resorts. During ski season, major ski resorts in the South Shore area provide free shuttle service daily (during ski season) to and from motels, hotels, lodges and numerous designated roadside stops. Year-round area shuttle bus service and low-cost trolleys and taxis are widely available.

68| Golfing in Lake Tahoe

Lake Tahoe boasts a dozen championship golf courses and a spring, summer or fall golf vacation rental is a great getaway for guys, gals and couples. (Area courses close for the winter season.) And, you may play the best game of your life. Adjust your swings and putts; they say balls go farther at the 6,200 foot altitude. Settle into your Lake Tahoe vacation rental and head for the greens.

To the south, **Lake Tahoe Golf Course** boasts being Tahoe's best championship golf value. Located in a mountain meadow surrounded by the High Sierras, this par 71 spectacular golf course challenges all levels. Green fees are seasonal ranging from $41-$74. **The Tahoe Paradise Golf Course** is a relaxing 18-hole executive course with affordable greens fees of $27-$57.

Want to play the most upscale course in Lake Tahoe? Get ready to hand over $250 in green fees at **Edgewood Tahoe**. Toward the North, **The Incline Village Championship** and **Incline Village Mountain**, both designed by Robert Trent Jones, demand accuracy and creativity with challenging play against a breathtaking mountain backdrop.

69| Lake Tahoe Never Sleeps

If indoor action and hot nightlife are important, a South Lake Tahoe vacation rental near the "border" in Stateline is a good choice. **Harrah's, Harvey's, Horizon and MontBleu** are the leading South Lake Tahoe razzle-dazzle casinos. **Bill's Casino** draws a more laid-back party crowd and **Lakeside Inn & Casino** is a low-key favorite with Lake Tahoe locals. Away from the gaming tables, South Lake Tahoe nightclubs include: *Attitude*, voted the "Best of Tahoe;" *blu,* a high-tech club in MontBleu and *Cabo Wabo*, Sammy Hagar's club that draws unannounced celebrity entertainment and nightly promotions.

70| Ski Vacations in Lake Tahoe

There are many accolades for Lake Tahoe ski resorts. Online, Travelzoo recently named Lake Tahoe a "Top 10 Ski Resort Choice" and *Skiing* magazine consistently ranks Lake Tahoe to their Top 25 Resorts. Whether you are a beginning, intermediate or expert skier, there's a ski resort waiting in Lake Tahoe. If you prefer alpine or cross-country skiing, it's there. And, off the slopes there's sledding, snowmobiling, snowshoeing, ice-skating, sleigh rides and year-round fishing.

With 18 area ski resorts, Lake Tahoe claims the largest concentration of ski resorts of any U.S. ski destination. Ski resorts range from tiny north lake **Granlibakke** (a one lift resort primarily for beginning skiers) and **Soda Springs** with two lifts and $25 lift tickets to upscale **Heavenly Mountain Resort** in the south with 30 lifts, ski trails and $72 ski lift tickets. **Kirkwood Resort** and **Sierra at Tahoe** are also popular South Tahoe ski venues. **Squaw Valley, Northstar** and **Alpine Meadows** are popular North Lake Tahoe Resorts.

If cross-country skiing is your game, look at resorts like: **Kirkwood Ski Resort**, **Northstar** and **Royal Gorge Cross-Country Ski Resort**. Return to the warmth and privacy of your personal vacation home rental after an exhilarating day on the slopes. Prepare dinner and enjoy the camaraderie of sharing stories of the day around the table before heading out to a local casino for a night of gambling and entertainment. Or, imagine a romantic dinner and evening for two in front of a crackling fire in our cozy condo or ski chalet and create your own entertainment.

71| Viva Las Vegas

There is no city in the world like Las Vegas. A Las Vegas vacation is all about fun and fantasy. It's a trip around the world. Only in Vegas can you see a collage of larger than life replicas of the Eiffel Tower, a Sphinx, a Roman Forum and the Statue of Liberty...just to name a few of Vegas' most famous landmarks.

Only in Vegas can you experience an erupting volcano, pirates battling playgirls, western shoot-outs, dare-devil circus acts and the best people-watching on the planet long a three or four mile strip. A Vegas vacation is guaranteed to entertain and enthrall. Win a fortune and lose it again in less than one hour. Catch a performance by today's hottest stars like Elton John or Celine Dion or a performance by stars of yesterday like the Sammy Davis or Elvis Presley. "Hey Honey, are you *sure* that guy isn't the *real* Elvis?" Often called Sin City, Las Vegas is a contradiction of experiences.

It's glitzy and gaudy; tacky and terrific; eccentric and exciting. Here's a surprising bit of Vegas trivia: There are more churches per capita in Sin City than in any other city in America . One thing for sure; vacation rentals in Vegas are never boring!

72| What's Happening in Las Vegas

Research and planning are important parts of successful travel. The Internet offers a goldmine of Las Vegas travel resources. Find the perfect Las Vegas vacation home rental. Compare vacation rental properties and amenities. Read reviews from previous vacation renters. See what you are getting before you book by browsing photographs of vacation rental homes. Use location maps to choose a vacation rental in the most convenient location.

Visit Websites of the Las Vegas Convention and Visitors Authority, the Las Vegas Chamber of Commerce and the Nevada Commission on Tourism for up-to-date and accurate information about area attractions and current events. Plan your itinerary before you leave home, but save some time for surprises and spontaneity. When you arrive at your Las Vegas rental, pick up brochures, tourist publications and local newspapers with local calendars of events and discount coupons.

73| Exciting Las Vegas Day Trips

Away from the crowds along the Strip, there are Las Vegas vacation home rentals nestled in nature that are within a short drive to some of America's greatest natural wonders. Outside of the neon landscape of Vegas, there are breathtaking desert, canyon and mountain landscapes waiting to be discovered. Grab a guidebook and a map and head out in your rental car or book an organized tour. Here are some day trip ideas for your Las Vegas must-see-must-do list:

- **Valley of Fire State Park** is located about one hour northeast of Las Vegas. It derives its name from incredible red sandstone formations formed by the shifting sand dunes during the age of the dinosaurs. Sites of interest within the park include: Arch Rock, Beehive formations, Elephant Rock, Mouse's Tank, Rainbow Vista. Seven Sisters and Poodle Rock. Look for examples of ancient Indian art on Atlatl Rock.
- **See the Grand Canyon** without the 300 mile drive. Scenic Airlines runs deluxe guided air and ground tours that include a flight over the canyon, a bus excursion through the park and lunch. Tour prices start at $219 for an experience that is sure to be a highlight of your vacation.
- **Visit Hoover Dam.** Located 30 miles southeast of Las Vegas at the Nevada-Arizona border, Hoover Dam has been hailed as "the Eighth Wonder of the World." The engineering marvel stands 736 feet high, 1,244 feet wide at its crest, and is 660 feet thick at its base with enough concrete in its structure to pave a highway across the United States. Two guided tours leave at regular intervals throughout the day.

74| Family Friendly Las Vegas

You may be surprised to discover that Las Vegas is not just for grown-ups. According to the Las Vegas Convention and Visitors Authority, there are around 400 family-oriented shows and activities in and around the city. Here's a sample of some Vegas fun the whole family:

- Watch the dare-devil acts at Circus-Circus or spend an entire day in the Adventuredome indoor theme park.
- Take to the animals at the Wildlife Habitat at the Flamingo or the Lion Habitat at the MGM Grand.
- See the dazzling 54-foot high volcano eruption at the Mirage every 15 minutes from dusk until midnight.
- Go behind-the-scene at Ethel M's Chocolate Factory. Free samples!
- Learn about life in the West and the desert at Marjorie Barrick Museum of Natural History.
- Catch a performance at the Las Vegas Comedy Pet Theatre. Popovich's show features a wild and heart-warming mixture of comedy, juggling skills and animal acts.
- Get a bird's eye view from atop the Stratosphere Tower, the tallest building in the America West. On a clear day, you can see Arizona and California. At night, the neon lights of Vegas come alive.

Las Vegas vacation home rentals are also family friendly. Instead of sharing an expensive, cramped hotel room, a family of four or more can enjoy privacy and all the comforts of home and more.

75| Getting Around Las Vegas

If you only plan to stay on the Strip and spend your days on in-door pursuits, you probably won't need a car in Las Vegas. McCarran International Airport is close to the city and a taxi ride to the Strip runs about $12-$15. Once settled, a sleek high-tech monorail whisks visitors between hotel casinos along the Strip for $3 one-way.

Many hotels also offer complimentary trams service between casinos or you can don your most comfortable walking shoes and take in the sights on foot. However, if your vacation rental is away from the Strip and when you are ready to escape the neon for nature, a rental car allows you the freedom to set your own pace. As in most major cities, car rental rates vary depending on the rental period and type of car.

Several major airlines like Delta and American Airlines offer special Fly & Drive packages with savings on combining airfare and car rental. Use Internet resources to make comparison shopping easy. Save on rental rates with AAA, AARP and airline frequent flyer partnerships. Check daily versus weekly rates. Look for rentals with unlimited miles if you plan to explore some of the popular attractions outside the city.

Heads up: Las Vegas is a compact city and traffic at peak times is heavy. Avoid bumper-to-bumper traffic by parking toward the end of the Strip and using the monorail or trams. Don't worry about parking, many of the casino hotels offer free valet service and there are self-parking lots nearby.

76| Getting Married or Divorced in Las Vegas

Las Vegas is known for wild and wacky, and ritzy and romantic weddings. Over 120,000 couples wed in Las Vegas each year. Some weddings are planned months in advance; while other weddings are "spontaneous" events.

Prices for elegant ceremony at the Bellagio start at $1,500 and rise accordingly. The Little White Chapel is probably the best-known venue for a quickie wedding. You can get married at the Elvis Wedding Chapel by an Elvis look-a-like. You can wed between poker hands in a casino. You can say your vows in the Tunnel of Love Drive-Thru Chapel with special rates for bikers. Get married in privacy at poolside or in the spa at your Las Vegas vacation home rental.

No matter what wedding you chose, if you it to be legal, get a marriage license at the Clark County Courthouse. It's open seven days a week from 8 a.m. until midnight.

On the other hand, the reputation for a "quickie" 24-hour divorce Las Vegas is a myth. If you meet the guy or gal of your dreams during your vacation, you can't get married one night and divorced the next morning.

For a legal divorce in Nevada, you or your spouse must be a full-time resident of Nevada for at least six total weeks before commencement of the action according to Nevada Statute NRS 125.020. Beware of companies offering a "simplified" divorce with no residency. Just as a marriage requires a license to be legal, a divorce must meet residency requirements or it is not legal in all 50 states.

77| Las Vegas Special Interest Freebies

You can easily spend $200 on a single show or round of golf in Las Vegas; however, there are also many fun and fascinating freebies for all ages interests near your vacation rental. The **Bellagio Conservatory** is a glass-domed 90,000 square foot conservatory filled with over 1,200 kinds of exotic plants and flowers. Displays are changed monthly. Admission is free. Ron Lee's **World of Clowns** offers a free self-guided factory tour. Wine lovers can enjoy free tours and wine tasting at the **Pahrump Valley Vineyards.** Car buffs get revved up at the **Shelby American Inc**. sports car museum featuring the latest version of Shelby American sports vehicles and a dozen Cobra cars. Free tours of the assembly area are offered Monday-Friday at 10 a.m.

Stoogie aficionados can take a free tour of the **Don Pablo Cigar Company**. The **Lost City of Atlantis** Show at Caesars delights friends of the sea. There's a 50,000 gallon saltwater aquarium and shows daily at 11 am. The **Fremont Street Experience** is a free one-of-a-kind light and sound show. Over two million lights are projected on a massive canopy stretching over 1,400 feet along Main Street to Fourth Street accompanied by 100,000 watts of sound. Come for the show and stay for the fun. Get the idea? There's more than gambling in Vegas.

78| Vegas Tips for Novice Gamblers

Although there are many reasons to visit Las Vegas besides gambling; few visitors can resist the lure of the tables and slots. From penny slots to million dollar high-roller stakes, Las Vegas offers just about every gambling option known to man. Casinos are open 24 hours a day. Sometimes Lady Luck smiles and sometimes she turns on you. Vegas veterans offer these tips:

- Set your limits. Determine your gambling budget before your arrive in Vegas and stick to it. Gambling is not a way to make money. Don't bet the farm in an effort to win.
- Play at the right casino. All casinos are not the same. Check out casinos until you find one that has the atmosphere you enjoy.
- If you are a novice gambler, practice playing early morning when tables are not crowded.
- Start small. Choose table play with low minimum plays so that you don't loose your cash too quickly.
- If and when you double your money, stash your original gambling funds and play on your winnings.

- Get the most "bang" for your buck by joining players' clubs. Most major Las Vegas casinos have a "club" you can join and earn rewards like free dining or merchandise based on how much money you spend. It's free to join, but you must register and receive a player's card that tracks play electronically.
- Enjoy the free cocktails, but don't over-imbibe and let alcohol dull your judgment.
- Play the games you enjoy most and join in the camaraderie. Cheer for the winners and commiserate with the losers. Have fun!

Return to your Las Vegas vacation home rental at the end of the day. Relax, recoup and revive. Tomorrow's another day of fun and fantasy in Vegas.

79| When to Go (and Not to Go) to Las Vegas

Las Vegas is a year-round destination, but the weather is not the same year-round. Inside the casinos, the weather is always the same, but outdoors the weather can change dramatically with the seasons. Typical of desert environments, summer daytime weather is very hot and dry, but temperatures drop 20 or more at night. Winter brings nighttime temperatures near freezing, but days are temperate.

In January, a Las Vegas visitor can ski the Mount Charleston's slope in the early morning and water- ski at Lake Mead in the same day. Las Vegas residents say the best seasons in Las Vegas are late spring and early fall. Las Vegas crowds and prices skyrocket during holidays and when large conventions come to town. Las Vegas is a major convention destination with many conventions topping the 100,000 mark in attendance. It pays to check convention schedules with the Las Vegas Convention and Visitors Authority before booking your Las Vegas vacation. Although you can escape the crowds to your vacation rental, the casinos, shows and restaurants are mobbed during major conventions. If you are not part of the convention, avoid doing Vegas during convention periods.

80| Why Stay in a Las Vegas Vacation Rental?

In a city where the hotels are attractions, why stay in a vacation rental? Glad you asked. The old days of cheap Las Vegas vacations are gone. Hotels, restaurants and entertainment cost more. Want to see Celine Dion, Barry Manilow or one of Cirque du Soleil's performances? Prepare to drop as much as $200 per person. Looking for a free buffet? You may find a few, but don't expect mountains of shrimp and tender steaks; you get what you pay for. Want to stay at a luxury hotel like Caesar's Palace? Prepare to pay $240-$350 per night for a room and $700 or more per night for a suite.

On the other hand, there are hundreds of Las Vegas vacation home rentals ranging from fully-equipped studios and condos right on the Strip to palatial estates nearby with savings of 40% or more over hotel stays. Imagine a 7,500 square foot luxury mansion with 14 bedrooms, an Olympic-sized private pool and spa, high-tech entertainment center, gourmet kitchen and park-sized backyard for you and 20 or so close friends. At $950 per night, 10 couples can live in luxury for $95 per night. Vegas is all about living large! Action on the Strip is exciting, but 24-hours on the Strip can be too much of a good thing. A vacation rental let's you take advantage of all the excitement and unplug from the action when you are ready. And, you can use money you save on your vacation rental to splurge on an extravagant show. Save dining dollars by preparing some meals in your own kitchen and treat yourself to a few special nights out at one of Las Vegas' top restaurants. You can live large for a lot less with a little planning and preparation.

81| Choosing a Ski Vacation Rental Destination

No two ski destinations are the same. Consider these factors when researching potential ski vacation rental destinations:

- **Resort Demographics:** Some ski resorts are family-oriented; others cater to singles and couples-only. Some ski destinations offer a bounty of attractions and activities off the slopes; others are all about the ski experience. Check the stats on current weather and ski slope conditions. It's no secret that ski resorts are cold. However, some mountains are colder than others and some slopes require more endurance to rugged elements.
- **Personal Ski Levels**: Some ski resorts are not suitable for beginners; others are not challenging enough for expert skiers. If your ski group is mixed, opt for ski resorts that offer opportunities for all skill levels.
- **Your Travel Budget**: Like golf, skiing is not a "poor man's sport." That said, ski vacations run the gamut from luxury to affordable. Top-of-the-line ski equipment and the trendiest togs don't come cheap, but there are ways to look the part without breaking your budget.

The best ski destination is one that matches your personal needs, expectations and budget. Continue on for more information on using these factors to plan the perfect ski vacation.

82| Colorado Ski Vacation Rentals

Colorado offers some of the best ski resorts in North America and is home to high profile ski destinations like Aspen, Breckenridge and Vail. **Aspen Snowmass** is actually four resorts in one - Snowmass, Aspen Mountain, Aspen Highlands and Buttermilk. Each mountain has advantages. For instance:

Buttermilk is geared towards beginner and intermediate skiers with wide-open trails. Vacation home rentals range from an affordable cozy studio for two for as low as $450 per week to living like the rich and famous in a grand estate featuring five or more bedrooms and loads of amenities for $25,000 per week.

Breckenridge has a lot of terrain for beginners to pros, and plenty to do on and off the slopes. It is also part of the Vail Resorts 5 mountain season pass that allows locals to ski at five resorts for the season for $369 (Unlimited skiing at A-Basin, Keystone, Breckenridge and 10 days at Vail/Beaver Creek).

Vail offers a complete ski experience on and off the slopes. As the "grand daddy of Colorado ski resorts," Vail is consistently named one of the top resorts in the U.S.

Travelers considering a Colorado vacation rental should also take a look at these somewhat less acclaimed, affordable and often less crowded ski resorts: Arapohoe Basin, Arrowhead Ski Area, Beaver Creek, Berthoud Pass, Copper Mountain, Crested Butte, Durango Mountain Keystone, Loveland, Monarch, Powderhorn, Sunlight, Telluride and Winter Park.

83| Canadian Ski Vacation Rentals

Canada is a skier's Mecca and ski vacation rentals are as diverse as ski venues. Choose your experience from beginners and family skiing, to challenges best suited for experts. In Alberta, Banff National Park is home to the Banff /Lake Louise/Sunshine Village ski area. The park is designated as a UNESCO World Heritage Site. It is no wonder that the area is consistently rated by major ski magazines as having some of best scenery in North America. Nearby, Canmore is known for some of the best cross-country skiing and the wildest skiing in Canada. Jaspar/Marmot Basin offers 84 named trails for downhill skiing. The terrain is designated 30% for beginners, 30% intermediate and 40% expert.

In British Columbia, Whistler/Blackcomb's majestic mountain scenery and spectacular array of ski and non-ski activities draw visitors from around the world. Whistler/Blackcomb offers over 8,000 acres of terrain with more than 200 marked trails. The resort is known for a top-notch ski school with group and private lessons for all skill levels, including specialty classes for disabled skiers. Looking for high adventure and rugged skiing? Kicking Horse Mountain Resort in the Purcell Range of the Canadian Rockies (two and a half hours west of Calgary) is surrounded by six national parks and offers some of the exciting and challenging skiing in North America.

84| European Ski Vacation Rentals

For a luxury ski vacation look at famous Alps peaks like: Eiger, Jungfrau and Matterhorn. Switzerland vacation rentals offer the advantages of skiing long, scenic runs combined with snowshoeing, snowboarding, dog sledding, tobogganing, ice climbing, and horse-drawn sleigh rides. Take advantage of winter discounted airfares and treat the whole family to an Alpine ski vacation at a ski-in and ski-out fully-equipped Swiss Ski Lodge.

Ski Austria. An Austria vacation rental offers magnificent mountains, music, arts and architecture and a thriving nightlife. Reserve a breathtaking view with your Austria vacation rental in Innsbruck, combining Old World charm with modern day skiing for all levels of ski enthusiasts. Ski with the rich and famous at one of the most famous ski resorts in the world, Mont-Blanc.

Ski Italy. The Aosta Valley contains the most mountains in all of Italy. Hop abroad a train and extend your ski vacation to Tuscany wine country, see the glories of Rome and Florence or fall in love with Venice .

85| Saving Money on a Ski Vacation

If money is no object when it comes to ski vacations, skip this topic; however, if you want the best experience for the best price, read on for ways to save on and off the slopes.

- **Choose a low-profile ski destination.** If you have your heart on skiing with the rich and famous in a high-profile, upscale resorts like Aspen, St. Moritz or Mont-Blanc offer the height of luxury with a price to match. On the other hand, Copper Mountain and Winter Park are Colorado ski vacation rental locations where you can experience top-notch skiing at a reasonable price. In the northeast, check out ski resorts and vacation rentals in Maine, upstate New York and Vermont.
- **Rent ski gear.** If this is your first ski trip and you are not sure skiing is for you and your family, rent ski equipment. Research rentals online at your ski destination to avoid having to juggle the logistics of travel with ski gear. (Note: Renting ski gear for young children is always smart move. They almost always outgrow last year's gear before the next ski trip.) Spend a few dollars more for the latest equipment; it's safer and easier to use. Take out damage insurance for adult and kid's gear...just in case something goes awry. If you must have your own gear, look at secondhand gear from a reputable sports equipment retailers.

- **Book accommodations at a ski vacation home rather than a pricey resort.** A vacation rental cabin, chalet or condo is ideal for a family or group of friends. No sharing a single room. No waiting for the bathroom. Two families or a group of friends sharing the cost of a ski vacation home average saving 30% or more on accommodations alone. A day on the slopes builds big appetites. Save more by stocking up on snacks at a local grocery and preparing your own meals in a fully-equipped kitchen. Picture the fun of gathering around the cozy fireplace to rehash the day and plan tomorrow or soaking away aches and pains in a steamy hot tub under the starlit sky.
- **Avoid high demand ski times.** Plan your ski vacation rental for off-peak times at the beginning or end of the ski season for discounted prices. Ski mid-week for discounted lessons and lift tickets. Check for online lift ticket specials. Multi-day sky lift tickets are less than purchasing on a daily basis. Search Convention and Visitors Centers at your destination for online local discounts and promotions.

86| Researching Ski Vacation Rentals

The newsstands are filled with ski and outdoor publications like ***Ski Magazine*** and ***Skiing*** that are packed with information about various types of resorts for skiers, where to dine, what to do off the slopes and tips from the pros. There are also numerous books on skiing. For starters, check out ***The Best Family Ski Vacations in North America, Fodor's Skiing USA*** and ***100 Best Ski Resorts of the World.*** The Internet is also a great resource for researching potential ski destinations and ski vacation rentals. Narrow your search with phrases that incorporate your personal interests such as: "Colorado vacation rentals" or "best family ski vacation destinations."

Finally, ask around. Veteran ski enthusiasts live for ski season. They've been-there, done-that and are happy to share their experiences. Enter search words "ski resort reviews" for hundreds of reviews on major online travel agency sites like: Travelocity, Travelzoo and Sidestep.

87| Ski Resort Fun for Non-Skiers

Not everyone enjoys the exhilaration of flying down a ski slope. If the whole family or all of your friends dream of a ski vacation, take heart. The key to fun for a non-skier is choosing a ski vacation rental with non-skiing and in-door entertainment options.

- Snow tubing is one of the latest rages at resorts. Instead of perching on a pair of skis, lower your center of gravity and whisk down the slope seated. Everyone can do it...no lessons needed, no expensive equipment to purchase...just have fun!
- Bundle up the gang for an old-fashioned sleigh ride complete with hot chocolate or hot buttered rum.
- Just not the outdoor type? Opt for pampering at an area day spa, shop 'til you drop at outlet malls, galleries and specialty boutiques.
- Curl up by the fireplace with that novel you haven't been able to find the time to start. Make new friends in the ski lodge. There are always non-skiers hanging out and camaraderie makes for interesting conversations.
- Many resorts offer culinary classes and wine tasting. For instance, some Vermont ski resorts offer maple sugaring classes, antiquing excursions and art classes. And, when everyone else comes off the slopes, you'll be rested and ready for a night on the town.

88| Ski Utah Vacation Rentals

Within 60 miles of the Salt Lake City International Airport, 11 world-class ski resorts offer a not-to-be-missed ski experience. With over 152 flights arriving in Salt Lake City before noon, you can fly in the morning and be on the slopes by afternoon. Alta, Solitude and Brighton are all within half an hour of Salt Lake City and offer un-crowded skiing for the whole family.

Snowbird's famous tram whisks 125 skiers to the top of Hidden Peak in six minutes. It is also the location of the first ski tunnel in North America. Book a vacation ski rental in a luxury three-bedroom condo in Salt Lake City for as low as $1,000 for a week. Save even more with a **Salt Lake Super Pass** with discount skiing at multiple resorts. The Pass can be loaded with one to six days of skiing and redeemed for an all-day lift ticket at Alta, Brighton, Snowbird or Solitude. It also includes round-trip transportation on UTA city buses, ski resort buses and TRAX light-rail. **Park City** is just 35 minutes from the Salt Lake City Airport and is home to three more world-class resorts: **Deer Valley, The Canyons** and **Park City Mountain Resort**. And when you have your fill of the action on the slopes, explore the history and charm of this silver mining community.

From ski-in, ski-out luxury condominiums to cozy cabins for two to chalets for ten or more, Park City offers all the comforts of home and more in ski vacation rental choices.

89| Summer Ski Vacation Rentals

Ski destinations aren't just for winter. Summer at ski destinations brings a bounty of activities and affordable off-season vacation rental rates. Check out these family favorites destinations for your summer vacation:

- **Sun Valley, Idaho** is a premier winter ski destination, but summer provides plenty of nature to explore. Learn the intricacies of fly fishing or experience the thrill of rafting along the Salmon River. Hike flower filled mountain and valleys. Rollerblade along the Wood River Trail System. Recapture the gracious lifestyle and romance of bye-gone eras in a luxury chalet sleeping eight at 50% off ski-season rates. Breath-taking scenery is perfect for hiking, rock climbing, biking, golf, tennis, fishing, rafting, horseback riding, year-round ice skating including performances by Olympic and World Champions, shopping, fine dining, live theater, and more.
- **Telluride, Vail and Aspen** are known for serious winter skiing in Colorado, but summer brings a different kind of family fun. The surrounding peaks are ideal for hiking and biking and summer festivals and special events provide entertainment for all ages. Summer is the perfect time to reconnaissance potential winter ski destinations. Save 50% or more on Colorado vacation home rentals. Enjoy the outdoors and special events and check out area resort ski packages, lessons and accommodations for a winter ski vacation.

90| Tips on Ski Lessons

Ski lessons are a necessity for first-time skiers. Professional ski lessons teach the basics and vital safety guidelines. Research ski lessons online *before* booking a ski vacation home rental. Some destinations offer more ski school options than others. The Internet is great for research, but when it comes to ski lessons, call the resorts you are considering and ask these questions:

- Are lessons private or group lessons? Most ski resorts offer both private and group lessons. If you are comfortable learning with others, group lessons cost less and are fun, especially for children. Ask about class sizes. It is hard to get any personal attention in classes with over six students.
- What is included with the lessons? Do they include ski equipment and lift tickets?
- Are instructors certified? Look for instructors who specialize in working with children.
- Can classes be booked in advance? Ski lessons at popular resorts fill up fast.

91| A Picture is Worth a Thousand Words

Photographs add instant appeal to properties. Most vacation home renters hesitate to inquire about property not marketed with photographs. Give your vacation rental a proper photo shoot and tempt prospective guests with flattering photographs.

- Vacation rental photographs should include outside and inside views of your home.
- Take photographs outside on a sunny day during different seasons. If you have a ski rental, be sure that your photographs include snow scenes.
- For a warm and cozy interior look, light a fire in the fireplace; turn on lights and open curtains; place fresh flowers on tables or a bowl of fresh fruit on a kitchen counter.
- Photograph views from the windows of living areas and from balconies or patios. If you have a beach rental, catch the surf rolling in on a sunny day when the beach is *not* crowded.
- Include photographs of impressive d ecor such as a gourmet kitchen, master bath with garden tub/Jacuzzi or high-tech entertainment center.
- Don't take pictures of people in your condo. Let renters imagine a home for themselves, not someone else.

92| Attracting Off-Season Vacation Guests

Peak or high season vacation rental rates are the most profitable times for vacation rentals. In fact, many vacation rentals by owner are able to pay annual rental expenses and clear a healthy profit during a few months of peak season. A three-bedroom condo may rent for $3,000 a week during peak season in Florida, whereas off-season the going rate may only be $1800 per *month.* When off-season rolls around, don't give up your marketing efforts. Update your Website directory listings with seasonal appeals like photographs of beautiful fall foliage or snow-capped mountains and tips on seasonal local events. Decorate your vacation home rentals with seasonal touches such as a fall wreath or Christmas tree. If you don't have a gas fireplace, stock firewood for your guests.

Check out your competition. What are they offering to entice off-season rentals? Match them and go the extra mile. Offer off-season promotions and special deals. Highlight additional off-season savings at area attractions and restaurants. Smart planning and a little extra effort can turn off-season home rentals into a healthy addition to your annual bottom line of your vacation rental.

93| Common Mistakes in Renting Vacation Homes

The most common mistakes made by vacation rentals by owner are:

- Not having a financial "cushion" to handle vacancy periods and property up-keep.
- Neglecting to maintain property in perfect condition for peak rental cycles.
- Not hiring reliable cleaning and maintenance professionals.
- Failing to research online property listing opportunities.
- Not researching rental rates and under-pricing or over-pricing rentals.
- Using a poorly written rental agreement.
- Failing to carry sufficient homeowners/liability insurance.
- Underestimating the importance of rental amenities and property extras.
- Neglecting follow-up with renters.

Do your homework. Comprehensive research and attention to detail help property owners avoid mistakes and maintain successful rental track records.

94| Encouraging Return Guests and Getting Referrals

One of the oldest marketing truisms is that business success depends on repeat customers and referrals from delighted customers. This is also true in the world of vacation home rentals. Many vacation home renters become annual guests that you can count on to return to your property year after year. Research also shows that repeat renters are the guests you can count on to respect and care for your vacation home.

- Get to know your renters. Email is a great resource, but impersonal. Whenever possible, talk with prospective guests before their stay to answer questions and offer tips.
- Contact guests during their stay to ensure satisfaction.
- Send them a thank-you card immediately after their stay.
- Maintain a database of previous guests and send holiday greetings or a birthday card.
- Email "previous guests only" offers from time to time.
- Acknowledge returning guests with a small gift of appreciation.

When it comes to referrals, statistics show that even sales professional neglect to ask for referrals from satisfied customers 95% of the time. Yet, referrals are of the most powerful marketing tools. Provide on-site information about your vacation home rentals and encourage guests to share them with their friends. Offer incentives for referrals such as a discount on future rentals for referrals.

95| Enhance Rental Property Listings

The Internet has revolutionized vacation rental marketing. Competition for rentals is stiff as thousands of new vacation rentals by owner pop up online every week. It is important to stand out from the crowd. It pays to do your homework and know your competition. Spend some time online searching vacation rentals similar to your property. Note what appeals to you and what turns you off.

- Choose words that appeal and get results when describing your vacation rental. Avoid over-used words like "big, beautiful and best." Marketing experts suggest using words that appeal to prospective guests' basic needs and emotions like: clean, cozy, classic, traditional, luxurious, spacious, private, romantic, inviting and safe/secure. Of course, everyone's favorite word is "free." What can you offer of value to prospective guests that is *free*?
- Pin-point one-of-a-kind or unique aspects of your vacation home.
- Make it easy for prospective guests to contact you with questions or concerns and respond to inquiries as quickly as possible. A delay of days or even hours in responding to inquiries usually results in lost rentals.

96| Enhance Your Vacation Home

Vacation home renters want all the comforts of home...and more! If you're the owner of a vacation rental, it pays to invest in furnishing your rental with not only the basics, but with luxury touches not found in the average home. Most vacation rentals include the usual major kitchen appliances, but what about the many extras like a set of bar tools, a coffee grinder, a blender or waffle maker? Bedrooms and baths offer great opportunities to stand out from the masses. Picture a bed draped with romantic netting, high-count linens and piled high with cushy pillows. Stock the bathroom with large fluffy towels, decorator touches and a welcome set of upscale bath amenities.

Don't forget the outdoors! A gas grill on the patio and an outdoor dining area around a pool or hot tub always draw praise from your guests. And, don't forget to look for ways to make your vacation home more kid-friendly and kid-proof, and more accessible to physically-challenged guests. Study decorating and outdoor landscaping magazines for ideas that would make you say "WOW" in a vacation home. Ask your guests for suggestions or improvements that would add value to future stays.

97| Improving Vacation Home Care

There are horror stories about property abuse by vacation renters. But there several things you can do to encourage better property care from your vacation home renters and preventive maintenance to improve the daily wear and tear on your home. Get a head start during renovation and decorating, or whenever refurbishing is needed. Rather than selecting the least expensive, lowest-grade appliances and furnishings, wall and floor covering, choosing high or commercial grade choices that are tough and easy-care will pay-off in the long run.

For instance, a self-cleaning oven is a must. And, in Florida beach vacation homes, tile floors stand the test of time and sand better than carpet. Keep a reliable handyman on-call for emergency repairs. Stock basic home repair tools to encourage guests to solve their own small problems. No vacation home rental should be without a plunger, a screwdriver, mop, broom and flashlights. A file of owner's manuals for appliances and electronics reduces frustration and encourages guests to use them properly. Don't neglect preventive maintenance. A smoke detector, carbon monoxide detector and fire extinguishers are musts.

Repeat rentals and referrals will suffer when property begins to look worn and tired or if it is not properly cleaned. Most vacation rental owners schedule some "downtime" for repairs and touch-up after each season. Finally, ensure that your rental agreement is comprehensive in addressing damage deposits, especially if you are renting to families with children or pets. Encourage guests to bring any problems to your attention and respond with urgency.

98| Little Things Mean a Lot in Vacation Home Rentals

Once your vacation home is fully-furnished spend a "little extra for little things" that pay big returns in vacation home repeat rentals and referrals. Examples of little touches that never fail to impress include:

- A folder of area guides, maps, menus and discount coupons.
- A basket of microwave popcorn and granola bars.
- A first-day supply of coffee and hot tea.
- A collection of DVDs and CDs or coupons for a free local rental.
- A bookshelf with novels, paperbacks and guidebooks.
- A list of emergency numbers.
- Sample sizes of bath amenities.
- A first aid kit.

Maintain a checklist of extras and arrange for restocking with your cleaning service.

99| Marketing Your Vacation Home Rental

There are several avenues for marketing vacation rentals by owner. You can list your property with a local real estate management company. However, you will have to give up 20%-40% of rental fees to the management company. You can create your own vacation rental Website. However, unless you are a Webmaster, you will have to pay someone to create and maintain your site and unless you also pay a Web marketing company to draw traffic to your site, you will find the world does *not* beat a path just because you are "on the Internet."

Or, you can list your vacation rental by owner with one or more professional online vacation rentals directories. To find a vacation rental directory, search online for "vacation rental directories" or "vacation rentals by owner."

Look for vacation rental directory and rental sites that:

- Charge an annual fee rather than a rental percentage.
- Offer discounts for multiple property listings.
- Are user-friendly for owners and prospective renters.
- Allow 24/7 changes and ability to upload property photos.
- Include availability calendars.

- Allow contact with prospective renters by Email and telephone.
- Offer references from current vacation home owners.
- Feature page view and Email tracking statistics.
- Provide spam protection.
- Allow you to test the market with a free trial listing and money back trial period guarantee.

Successful, long-time vacation property owners advise listing vacation rentals by owner with at least three diverse online directories for maximum exposure.

100| Why Rent Your Vacation Home?

Vacation homes are gaining popularity every year. Maybe you are a Baby Boomer nearing retirement and considering a home in a dream location. Maybe you inherited a family vacation home that you want to keep, but would like to off-set the expenses and supplement income. Maybe you want investment property that you can rent while waiting for property values to increase for future resell. These are just a few scenarios that entice real estate owners to put their property on the vacation rentals by owner market. There are also tax advantages to vacation property rentals. Most vacation homeowners qualify for the same tax benefits traditional property landlords enjoy. Some of the factors to research when considering renting your vacation home include:

- How often do you want to use your vacation home? Personal use is limited when claiming rental deductions on your income tax
- How often do you want to rent your vacation home?
- How will you get the word out about your vacation rental?
- How will you handle the logistics of inquiries, bookings, cleaning, maintenance, and rental problems?

It pays to consult an attorney specializing in real estate rentals and a certified professional accountant to ensure that you reap the rewards and minimize the risks of rental property ownership.

101| Questions to Ask About Vacation Rentals

Look and ask before you book. You will find the answers to many questions on vacation rental Websites, but it still pays to talk to the property owner in person. Here are some vacation rental details you should know before booking:

• Total cost of the rental, including any "hidden or extra fees" like: charges for local taxes, booking fees, cleaning fees, additional utility fees and telephone or Internet access.

• How much is the security deposit? What does the deposit cover and when will it be returned?

• Get a copy of rental policies in writing before committing to a rental.

• Look up the address of prospective home rentals to ensure convenient location and check out the local neighborhood.

• Obtain the owner's name, telephone number and e-mail address. Get specific instructions for obtaining property keys and driving instructions.

• Find out how maintenance problems are handled and the telephone number for emergencies.

• Ask if the home is professionally cleaned and what cleaning you are expected to do.

• Request a detailed list of what is included such as kitchen appliances, kitchenware, linens, outdoor amenities and entertainment systems.

More Titles in the LifeTips Book Series

101 Green Travel Tips
by Lisa Handiak

101 Baby Travel Tips
by Christina Chan

101 Screenplay Tips
by Alexis Niki

101 Entrepreneur Tips
by Susan Payton

Printed in the United States
78085LV00004B/7

9 781602 750036